Strindberg
Plays: Two

The Dance of Death, A Dream Play, The Stronger

'Strindberg has been released from his reputation as an interesting madman, and his plays have been increasingly recognised as works of beauty and psychological understanding.' *Observer*

This volume contains two of Strindberg's best known plays from the prolific years following his mental breakdown, known as his 'post-Inferno' period: the complete text of his expressionist masterpiece *A Dream Play* (1901), which he described as 'my most beloved play, child of my greatest pain'; and both parts of *The Dance of Death* (1900), a terrifying analysis of a tormented marriage: 'it leaves an astonishing, an almost unaccountable, impression of genius ... as a beggar's cloak full of holes may have a kind of majestic beauty when the wind fills it, so this broken drama, having unmistakably the winds of vision in it, has beauty and dignity and power' (*The Times*, 1928). Also included is his earlier short play *The Stronger* (1889), a fascinating study of the power of personality.

Michael Meyer's translations of Strindberg are highly respected and widely performed, and in 1964 they won him the Gold Medal of the Swedish Academy, the first time that award has ever been bestowed on an Englishman. Meyer has also provided introductions tracing the origins and background of each play. He is the author of a definitive biography of Strindberg and has written a critically acclaimed play about his life, *Lunatic and Lover*.

AUGUST STRINDBERG

Plays: Two

The Dance of Death
A Dream Play
The Stronger

Translated from the Swedish with introductions by
Michael Meyer

METHUEN DRAMA

METHUEN WORLD CLASSICS

3 5 7 9 10 8 6 4

This collection first published as a paperback original in Great Britain
in 1982 by Methuen London Ltd by arrangement with Secker and
Warburg Ltd
Reprinted in this corrected edition in 1991, reissued with a
new cover design 1993, 2000

Methuen Publishing Ltd
215 Vauxhall Bridge Road, London SW1V 1EJ

English translations and introductions copyright © 1964, 1971, 1973,
1975, 1991 by Michael Meyer

The right of Michael Meyer to be identified as the translator of these
works has been asserted by him in accordance with the Copyright, Designs
and Patents Act, 1988

Methuen Publishing Limited Reg. No. 3543167

A CIP catalogue record for this book
is available from the British Library

ISBN 0 413 49750 X

Printed and bound in Great Britain by
Cox and Wyman Ltd, Reading, Berkshire

Caution

Contents

Johan August Strindberg

22 January 1849	Born in Stockholm, the fourth child of a shipping merchant and his former maid-servant.
1853	His father goes bankrupt.
1862	His mother dies. The next year his father marries his housekeeper.
1867	Goes to Uppsala University, where he decides to become a doctor.
1869	Fails preliminary examination, leaves University and goes on the stage. Fails at that. Writes his first plays, *A Nameday Gift* and *The Freethinker*.
1870	Returns to Uppsala to study modern languages and political science. His fourth play, *In Rome*, is performed briefly at the Royal Theatre in Stockholm.
1872	Leaves Uppsala and settles in Stockholm. Tries to go on the stage again, and fails again. Writes first major play, *Master Olof*, but it is not performed for nine years.
1872–4	Journalist in Stockholm.
1874–82	Librarian in Stockholm.
1877	Marries Finnish actress Siri von Essen.
1879	Established himself as an author with autobiographical novel, *The Red Room*.
1880–2	Writes historical and pseudo-historical prose works; also *The New Kingdom*, a provocative book for which he is venomously attacked.
1883	Leaves Sweden (partly because of these attacks) to spend the next six years abroad in France, Switzerland, Germany and Denmark. First theatrical success with *Lucky Peter's Journey* (his ninth play).

1884	Published volume of short stories, *Getting Married;* is prosecuted for blasphemy; returns to Sweden to face trial; is acquitted.
1886	Writes novel about his childhood, *The Son of a Servant.*
1887	Writes *The Father* in Bavaria. It has a small success in Denmark but fails in Sweden. Also writes rustic novel, *The People of Hemsö,* and, in French, *A Madman's Defence,* an account of his marriage.
1888	*The Father* staged by Freie Bühne in Berlin; Strindberg becomes known in Germany. He writes *Miss Julie* and *Creditors,* both in Denmark. *Miss Julie* attacked on publication for immorality.
1889	Starts own experimental theatre in Denmark; *Miss Julie* and *Creditors* are staged there, and fail. Theatre goes bankrupt. Strindberg returns to Sweden.
1891	Divorces Siri.
1892	Writes *Playing With Fire* and *The Bond,* his last play for six years. Leaves Sweden for Germany.
1893	Marries Austrian journalist, Frida Uhl. Visits England.
1893–7	Writes many pseudo-scientific articles for alchemistical and other journals, in French.
1894	Leaves Frida and settles in Paris. *Creditors* and *The Father* are staged there, and are well received. Strindberg is lionized but, as always, makes little money.
1894–6	Poor and alone in Paris. Scientific experiments; dabbles in alchemy and tries to make gold. *Inferno* crisis; hovers on brink of insanity.
1896	Emerges from mental crisis and returns to Sweden.
1897	Writes *Inferno* in French, the account of his years of near-madness.

1898	Writes Parts I and II of his dramatic trilogy, *To Damascus*. In the next eleven years he writes thirty-five plays.
1899	Writes *There Are Crimes and Crimes* and *Erik the Fourteenth*, his best historical play.
1900	Meets Norwegian actress, Harriet Bosse, twenty-nine years his junior. Writes *Easter* and *The Dance of Death*, Parts I and II.
1901	Writes *To Damascus*, Part III, and *A Dream Play*. Marries Harriet. She leaves him before the end of the year; returns briefly; then moves away for good (though they remain in contact).
1904–6	He writes no plays. His reputation in decline.
1907	Founds his own Intimate Theatre in Stockholm. Writes four chamber plays for it: *Storm*, *The Burnt House*, *The Ghost Sonata*, *The Pelican*, the first three all within ten weeks. They are coldly received.
1909	Writes last play, *The Great Highway*.
1909–12	Devotes last three years of his life to writing pamphlets on politics, sociology and philosophy.
14 May 1912	Dies in Stockholm of stomach cancer, aged sixty-three.

THE PLAYS OF STRINDBERG
(1849–1912)
with their dates of composition

PRE-INFERNO
1869 A Nameday Gift (lost)
     The Freethinker
1870 Hermione
     In Rome
1871 The Outlaw
1872–1877 Master Olof
1876–1877 Anno 48
1880 The Secret of the Guild
1882 Lucky Peter's Journey
     Sir Bengt's Wife
1886–1887 The Robbers (The
     Comrades)
1887 The Father
1888 Miss Julie
     Creditors
1888–1889 The Stronger
1889 Pariah
     The People of Hemsö
     Simoom
1892 The Keys of Heaven
     The First Warning
     Debit and Credit
     In the Face of Death
     A Mother's Love
     Playing with Fire
     The Bond

POST-INFERNO
1898 To Damascus, *Part I*
     To Damascus, *Part II*
     Advent
1899 There are Crimes and
     Crimes
     The Saga of the Folkungs
     Gustav Vasa
     Erik the Fourteenth

1900 Gustav Adolf
     Midsummer
     Casper's Shrove Tuesday
     Easter
     The Dance of Death,
     Part I
     The Dance of Death,
     Part II
1901 The Virgin Bride
     Swanwhite
     Charles XII
     To Damascus, *Part III*
     Engelbrekt
     Queen Christina
     A Dream Play
1902 Gustav III
     The Dutchman (frag-
     ment)
     The Nightingale of
     Wittenberg
1903 Exodus (Moses)
     Hellas (Socrates)
     The Lamb and the
     Beast (Christ)
1907 Storm
     The Burnt House
     The Ghost Sonata
     Toten-Insel (fragment)
     The Pelican
1908 The Last Knight
     Abu Casem's Slippers
     The Protector
     The Earl of Bjälbo
1909 The Black Glove
     The Great Highway

The Stronger

A Sketch
(1888–9)

Introduction to

THE STRONGER

STRINDBERG wrote THE STRONGER in December 1888-
January 1889, as part of the repertoire for his projected
Experimental Theatre in Copenhagen. Following upon
his row with Ludvig Hansen at Lyngby, his forcible expulsion
from the castle, and the publicity given in the Danish
newspapers to his affair with Hansen's seventeen-year-old
sister, Martha Magdalene, his relations with his wife had,
paradoxically, taken a turn for the better. She had stood by
him, partly perhaps because she was anxious not to lose this
opportunity of returning to the stage, and THE STRONGER is
one of the very few examples of Strindberg's work which
contains a sympathetic portrayal of his wife.

It was, like all his plays, based on fact. Since his marriage
he had had various flirtations with other women, including,
apart from Martha Magdalene, an actress named Helga
Frankenfeldt, who had formerly been employed at the Royal
Theatre in Stockholm, and Nathalia Larsen, the young
Danish actress and authoress who was to share the leads at
his experimental theatre with Siri. Siri seems not to have
been particularly jealous of these rivals, possibly because
they seemed the only means of diverting his own suspicions
away from her; and, after each affair, he came back to her.
"My friend and I are friends again—dear God, how tough
love is!", he wrote on 27 September 1888 to his cousin,
Johan Oscar Strindberg. At the time when he wrote this
little playlet, it must have seemed to him that his wife was,
after all, the strongest of all these women. The character of
Mademoiselle Y appears to have been chiefly based on
Helga Frankenfeldt, whom Strindberg had given up seeing
in 1882 after she had insulted Siri at a party.

He offered Siri the role of Madame X, but she refused it.
He then offered it to her rival, Nathalia Larsen, but she did
not like it either. "You haven't understood the play," he

13

wrote to her irritably on 7 January 1889. After unsuccessfully approaching two other actresses, including Johanne Krum who had played Laura in THE FATHER, he eventually succeeded in persuading Nathalia to accept the part: but in the end it was created by Siri. MISS JULIE was banned by the censor (see that Introduction in Strindberg *Plays: One*) on the day before the experimental theatre was to have opened, and THE STRONGER had to be hastily rehearsed with PARIAH to make up a triple bill the following week with CREDITORS. Nathalia was already fully occupied with rehearsing Tekla in the last-named play, and it was presumably thought that the strain of taking on another leading role would be too much for her. Mademoiselle Y was given to Fru Pio, who was acting Christine in MISS JULIE, and THE STRONGER received its first performance at the Dagmar Theatre in Copenhagen on 9 March 1889.

A few days before the première, Strindberg wrote Siri a few lines of advice concerning her part. As always, the precision and good sense of his remarks concerning practical theatrical details contrast amazingly with his hysteria on all other matters. "1. She is an actress, not just an ordinary respectable housewife. 2. She is the stronger, i.e. the softer. What is hard and stiff breaks, what is elastic gives and returns to its shape. 3. Poshly dressed—use the one you wore in MISS JULIE, or get something new. 4. If you get a new coat, beware of plain surfaces, and plain pleats, and buy a new hat! Something in fur, bonnet-shapped (not *à l'anglaise*). 5. Study it with meticulous care, but play it simply—but not too simply! Give it an undertone of 50% charlatanism, like Fru Hwasser* and Ibsen, and suggest depths that do not exist. 6. Change any phrases that don't come naturally, and work up to an exit that will bring applause, without making a meal of it. 7. Use your diaphragm when speaking, and don't squeak or rant. . . ."

None of the three plays was adequately performed, and the evening was less than a success. The critic of *Social-demokraten*, however, thought that Siri acted "with charm

*Elise Hwasser had played Nora in A DOLL'S HOUSE at the Royal Theatre in Stockholm in 1880.

and *noblesse*". Another observer noted that she "took repeated curtain-calls at the close of this *bagatelle*, which few people understood, but which they applauded because it was the end of the evening. Each time the curtain rose, it was she who stood upon the stage, and when there were calls for the author, who was not present, she addressed the audience, and promised to convey their greetings to him."

After the failure of the Experimental Theatre, THE STRONGER was forgotten until the turn of the century. As with so many of Strindberg's plays, it was Max Reinhardt who first realised and demonstrated its potential, with a production at his Kleines Theater in Berlin in 1902, in which Madame X was played by the distinguished actress Rosa Bertens. The play reached St. Petersburg in 1904 and Vienna in 1907, in which year it was played for the first time in Stockholm at Strindberg's own Intimate Theatre. It achieved the distinction of being the first Strindberg play to be performed in England, when the New Stage Club produced it at the Bloomsbury Hall on 29 November 1906 in a triple bill which also included Strindberg's playlet SIMOOM; and on 10 December 1909 it was revived at His Majesty's Theatre as curtain-raiser to a performance in Russian of Act 5 of Ostrovsky's IVAN THE TERRIBLE by Lydia Yavorskaia's company from St. Petersburg. Mlle Yavorskaia herself took the silent role of Mlle Y. in THE STRONGER, with Lady Tree as Mme X. Over the years, THE STRONGER has come to be recognised as a brilliantly effective curtain-raiser, and it has been frequently revived in Scandinavia, Germany and America.

Dr. Gunnar Ollén has suggested that Strindberg may deliberately have made one of the characters silent in the hope that his wife might be able to play that role in productions outside Sweden, notably, perhaps, at the Théâtre Libre in Paris, the director of which, André Antoine, had just expressed a strong enthusiasm for Strindberg's work. If so, Strindberg was not the only major dramatist to have written an important non-speaking role for this reason. Frau Helene Weigel once told me that when her husband, Bertolt Brecht, wrote MOTHER COURAGE in

Stockholm in 1938 he made the part of the Daughter dumb
in order that his wife might be able to play it in Sweden,
where he assumed it would receive its first production.
As things turned out, MOTHER COURAGE was not performed
in Sweden during Brecht's abbreviated stay there, and
Helene Weigel never played the part, although later of
course the Mother became her most famous role.

The Stronger

A Sketch
(1888–9)

This translation of THE STRONGER was broadcast on 1 May 1971 on London Weekend Television. The cast was:

MADAME X	Britt Ekland
MADEMOISELLE Y	Marianne Faithfull
WAITRESS	Ingrid Evans

Designed by Gordon Toms

Directed by Patrick Garland

CHARACTERS

MADAME X., a married actress
MADEMOISELLE Y., an unmarried actress
A WAITRESS

The corner of a café, of the kind frequented by ladies. Two small iron tables, a red plush sofa and some chairs. MADAME X. *enters in winter clothes, with hat and cloak, and a delicate Japanese basket on her arm.* MADEMOISELLE Y. *is seated with a half-empty bottle of beer in front of her, reading an illustrated magazine, which she later changes for others.*

MME X.: Why, Amelia darling! Fancy seeing you here! All alone on Christmas Eve, like a poor old bachelor!

MLLE Y. *looks up from her magazine, nods and goes on reading.*

MME X.: You know it really hurts me to see you like this. Alone – alone in a café – and on Christmas Eve! I remember once when I was in Paris – there was a wedding breakfast in a restaurant – and the bride sat there reading a comic paper while the bridegroom was playing billiards with the witnesses! My word, I thought, if they start like this, how will they go on – and how will they end? He was playing billiards on his wedding day! And she was reading a comic paper, you're going to say. Well, but it isn't quite the same

The WAITRESS *enters, places a cup of chocolate in front of* MME X. *and goes out.*

MME X.: You know what, Amelia? I really think you'd have done better to keep him. Don't you remember, I was the first person to say to you: "Forgive him!" Remember? You could have been married now, with a home. Do you remember last Christmas how happy you were with his parents in the country, and how you said that a happy home life was what really mattered, and that you'd like to get away from the theatre? Yes, Amelia,

21

my dear — home's best — after the theatre — and children, you know — no, of course, you don't.

MLLE Y. *gives her a disdainful glance.*

MME X. [*takes a few sips from her cup, then opens her basket and shows her Christmas presents*]: Look what I've bought for my little darlings! [*Takes out a doll,*] See this! This is for Lisa. Look — she can roll her eyes and turn her head! Mm? And this little pistol is for Maja.

She loads it, and fires the cork, on its string, at MLLE Y., *who recoils in fear.*

MME X. Did it frighten you? You thought I wanted to shoot you? Mm? Darling, you can't have! If *you'd* wanted to shoot *me*, I could understand — for getting in your way — I know you can never forget that — though it really wasn't my fault. You still think I got them to terminate your contract. But I didn't. I didn't, though you think I did. Well, it's no use my talking, you won't believe me. [*Takes out a pair of embroidered slippers.*] And these are for my dear husband. I embroidered these tulips myself. I hate tulips, but he will have them on everything.

MLLE Y. *looks up from her magazine, with cynical curiosity.*

MME X. [*puts a hand into each slipper*]: Look what small feet he has! Mm? And you should see how daintily he walks! But of course you've never seen him in slippers. [MLLE Y. *laughs aloud.*] Look, I'll show you! [*Walks the slippers along the table.* MLLE Y. *laughs aloud again.*] And then, darling, when he gets angry, he stamps his foot like this. "What! Damn these maids, will they never learn how to make coffee? Oh, God! Now the cretins haven't trimmed the lamp!" Or there's a draught under the door and his feet are cold. "Ugh, it's freezing! Can't these confounded idiots keep the stove alight!"

She rubs the sole of one slipper against the upper part of the other. MLLE Y. *roars with laughter.*

MME X. And then he comes home and can't find his

slippers, because Marie's hidden them under the chest of drawers. . . . Oh, but it's wicked to sit here and make fun of one's husband like this. He's a darling, actually – a real poppet! He's the kind of husband you ought to have had, Amelia! Why are you laughing? Mm? Mm? And then, you see, I know he's faithful to me. Oh, yes, I know. He told me himself – why are you giggling? – that when I was touring in Norway that horrid Frederique tried to seduce him! Can you imagine? The impertinence! [*Pause.*] I'd have scratched her eyes out if she'd shown her face while I was at home! [*Pause.*] It was lucky he told me about it himself. Imagine if I'd heard it from some gossip! [*Pause.*] But she wasn't the only one, you can be sure. I don't know why it is, but women always go crazy about my husband, They must think he has some pull at the theatre, because he works in the ministry. Perhaps you've been at him too! I was never quite sure about you – though I know now that he wasn't interested in you. I always felt you bore some grudge against him.

Pause. They look at each other uncertainly.

Mme X. Come and have dinner with us this evening, Amelia, to show you aren't cross with us – aren't cross with me, anyway. I think it's so horrid being bad friends with anyone – especially you. Perhaps it's because I queered your pitch that time. . . . [*Gradually slower.*] Or – I don't know – why – really – !

Pause. Mlle Y. gazes curiously at Mme X.

Mme X. It's so strange about our friendship – when I first met you, I was afraid of you, so afraid I didn't dare let you out of my sight. Wherever I went, I took care to be near you – I didn't dare become your enemy, so I became your friend. But I always felt awkward when you came home to us, because I saw my husband couldn't stand you – and then I felt uncomfortable, as though my clothes didn't fit. I did everything to make him be nice to you, but without success. And then you went off and got engaged. Then you and he became great friends – as

though you'd been afraid to show your true feelings while
you were uncommitted – and then – what happened next?
I didn't become jealous – funnily enough! And I remember,
when our first baby was christened, and you stood as
godmother, I made him kiss you – and he did, but you
got so upset – that is, I didn't notice it at the time – I
haven't thought of it since – haven't thought of it till –
now! [*Rises suddenly.*] Why are you so silent? You haven't
said a word all the time – you've just let me sit here
talking! you've sat there staring at me, winding all these
thoughts out of me like silk from a cocoon – thoughts –
suspicions – ? Let me see! Why did you break off your
engagement? Why did you never come and visit us after
that? Why won't you come and see us tonight?

MLLE Y. *seems about to speak.*

MME X.: No! You don't need to say anything – I see it all
now! So *that* was why you – and why you – and why
you—! Yes, of course! Now it all adds up! So that was
it! Ugh, I don't want to sit at the same table as you!

Moves her things to the other table.

That was why I had to embroider tulips, which I hate, on
his slippers – because you liked tulips! That was why –
[*throws the slippers on the floor*] – we had to spend our holiday
at Mälaren that summer, because you couldn't stand the
sea – that was why my son had to be called Eskil, because
that was your father's name – that was why I had to wear
your colours, read your authors, eat your dishes, drink your
drinks – your chocolate, for instance – that was why –
oh, my God! – it's horrible, now I think of it – horrible!
Everything, everything that belonged to you, entered into
me. Even your passions! Your soul crept into mine like a
worm into an apple, eating and eating, boring and boring,
till there was nothing left but skin and a little black
mould. I wanted to run away from you, but I couldn't –
you lay there like a snake with your black eyes, bewitching
me – when I tried to use my wings they dragged me
down. I lay in the water with my feet bound, and the

more I tried to swim with my hands the deeper I sank, down, down, till I reached the bottom, where you lay like a giant crab ready to seize me in your claws! And I'm lying there now!

Ugh, how I hate you, hate you, hate you! But you – you just sit there, silent, calm, not caring – not caring whether it's night or day, summer or winter, whether other people are happy or miserable – unable to hate and unable to love – motionless like a stork over a rat-hole! You couldn't pounce on your victim, you couldn't hunt it, but you could wait for it! You sit here in your corner – do you know people call it the rat-trap because of you? – and read your papers to see if anyone's in trouble, or ill, or has got the sack from the theatre – you sit here reckoning your victims, calculating your opportunities like a pilot counting his shipwrecks, like a goddess receiving sacrifice!

Poor Amelia! Do you know, I feel sorry for you, because I know you're unhappy – unhappy like someone who's been hurt – and evil because you've been hurt. I can't be angry with you, though I'd like to be – because you're the one who's the baby, not me. Oh, that business with Bob doesn't bother me – why should it? And what does it matter whether you taught me to drink chocolate, or someone else did? It's all one in the end.

Takes a sip from her cup. Continues knowingly.

Anyway, chocolate's very healthy! And if you've taught me how to dress – *tant mieux*! It's just made my husband fonder of me – your loss has been my gain. And to judge by certain signs, I think you have lost him. I suppose you hoped I'd run away? But you're the one who's run away – and now you're sitting here regretting it ever happened. But I don't regret it! One mustn't be petty. And after all, why should I want to own something that no one else wants?

You know, when all's said and done, perhaps I really am the stronger of us two; now anyway. You never took anything from me, you only gave. And now I'm like the thief in the fairy tale – when you woke, I had gone off with your treasure!

Otherwise why did everything become worthless and sterile as soon as you touched it? You couldn't keep any man's love, for all your tulips and your passions – as I have done. Your authors never taught you how to live; but they taught me. You never had any little Eskil; you only had a father called Eskil.

And why are you always silent, silent, silent? I used to think it was because you were strong; but perhaps it was just that you had nothing to say. Because your head was empty! [*Gets up and picks up the slippers.*]

Now I'm going home – and taking the tulips with me – *your* tulips! You couldn't learn anything from other people, you could only give – and so you broke, like a dry reed. But I didn't!

Thank you, Amelia, for all the good lessons you've taught me. Thank you for teaching my husband to love! Now I am going home, to love him.

She goes.

The Dance of Death

(1900)

STRINDBERG wrote Part I of THE DANCE OF
DEATH in October 1900, the same month in which
he wrote EASTER. The contrast between the two
plays is remarkable: EASTER is a play of reconciliation
and hope, THE DANCE OF DEATH an expression of the
blackest pessimism and hatred. But that he should have
written the two plays practically simultaneously is not as
incongruous as some critics have supposed. It was a part
of Strindberg's paranoid-schizophrenic character that he
alternated with bewildering rapidity between opposing
moods. Taken together, the two plays portray him more
accurately and fully than either work considered by itself.

After his return to Stockholm from Lund in the summer
of 1899, he had spent much time with his sister Anna and
her husband, Hugo Philp, a schoolmaster who had been a
fellow-student of Strindberg's at Uppsala thirty years before.
Philp had taken Strindberg's side in the family row of 1876
about the question of inheritance, as a result of which
Strindberg's father had excommunicated both Strindberg
and Anna; and he had also supported him in the contro-
versy surrounding the publication of Strindberg's short
stories, GETTING MARRIED, in 1884. Ten years later
Strindberg, turning suddenly against his old friend as
paranoiacs do, had written a spiteful character sketch
of Philp in a volume of scientific stories-cum-essays,
VIVISECTIONS; but the long-suffering Philps had visited
and consoled Strindberg during his INFERNO crisis in
Paris in 1896, and during this summer of 1899 they had
him to stay at their house at Furusund, in the Stockholm
archipelago. Their daughter Märta, as an old lady of over
ninety, told me her memories of this summer; how
Strindberg loved to sit in the evening sunlight with a glass
of wine and listen to her playing classical music on the
piano, "though he himself could only pick out a tune with

one finger". "He must have been a very difficult guest," I suggested, but she said: "No. He was charming, and so gentle." Then she was silent for a moment, and added: "Of course, when the black mood was on him, then he was terrible." Then another pause, and: "My mother was the same." She rebuked me for pronouncing his Christian name, August, in the French manner; she said it was always pronounced exactly like the month in English.

Anna had been trained as a violinist and had won a scholarship to Paris, but had declined it in order to marry Philp. Gunnar Ollén — whose admirable book, STRIND-BERGS DRAMATIK (Stockholm, 1961), so comprehensively details the factual background of the plays — describes her as having "a pronounced artistic temperament, like her brother", thus confirming her daughter's account of her, and as being "temperamental, restless and suspicious". Even when she was eighty, her motto was: "Peace and calm are the worst things I know." Märta tells that her mother was always moving, always travelling, loved parties, was impossible with servants and extravagant with money. Hugo Philp was a linguist and a wit, liked by his pupils. He adored his wife, though he was unfortunately totally unmusical. Intellectually and politically he was a radical, and remained sceptical about Strindberg's recent conversion to religion.

For about a year, things went well between Strindberg and the Philps. Anna, like Märta, would entertain him on the piano, and also the violin, and the family would play cards with him, which he enjoyed. In January 1900, Hugo became seriously ill with diabetes; Strindberg would sit with him, and they would talk about death. In May of that year Hugo had an attack of dizziness. At the beginning of June, Strindberg accompanied them, as in the previous year, to Furusund; but later that month he quarrelled with them, partly because Hugo defended some writers whom Strindberg loathed, partly because Hugo rebuked him for the way he had treated his first wife, Siri. Another reason seems to have been that Strindberg felt a strong physical attraction towards his sister, and was consequently jealous of Hugo. He was, moreover, suffering from a throat infection which increased his ill-humour, and before the end of June he returned angrily to Stockholm.

As was his custom when friends suddenly, in his eyes, became enemies, he conceived a violent hatred for Hugo, and his diary for that summer contains many references to Hugo and Anna. On 10 August, he noted: "Walked past the Philps' house [in Stockholm]. The blinds were down; on them were visible two hens tied by the necks, tugging at the cord, one on either side of an urn." When they celebrated their silver wedding on 5 October, Strindberg did not attend. Dr Ollén rightly remarks that anger tended to bring out the best in Strindberg as a writer, and that, recognizing this, he welcomed it and rejected attempts at reconciliation, at least until he had transmuted his anger into creative activity.

Four days later, on 9 October according to his OCCULT DIARY, he began THE DANCE OF DEATH, and by 31 October he had finished Part I — which, like Part I of TO DAMASCUS, he at first conceived as a complete play in itself, with no thought of a sequel. He took the title from Saint-Saëns' *Danse Macabre*, which he originally intended to include as the music to which the Captain dances; but, since Ibsen had used that in JOHN GABRIEL BORKMAN four years previously, Strindberg switched to *The Entry of the Boyars*. He told his German translator, Emil Schering, that he had considered entitling the play THE VAMPIRE. Although he wrote the play very rapidly, he had made several notes and sketches for it earlier; at various stages of its development, he planned to make the chief character a ship's pilot, a sacked professor and a hospital doctor. The play was probably influenced by Swedenborg's DE COELO ET INFERNO, a work which Strindberg knew well. In this, Swedenborg tells how happy a marriage can be when it "stands under the influence of religion"; but some marriages he states, "stand under the influence of evil"; and these are called "marriages of Hell". Partners in such a marriage can talk to each other, and may even be drawn to each other through lust; "but inwardly, they burn with a murderous mutual hatred which is so great that it cannot be described".

THE DANCE OF DEATH would seem to have been clearly based on the Philps. Alice is an actress who has given up her theatre career for marriage, just as Anna had sacrificed her musical career; Edgar, like Hugo, is suddenly taken seriously ill; and Kurt, who covets Edgar's wife, just as Strindberg seems secretly to have coveted Anna, sits by the bedside of the husband he would like to replace, and comforts him. Like the Philps, Edgar and Alice have a silver wedding coming up; they even share the Philps' liking for a game of cards. Hugo Philp certainly supposed Edgar to be based on himself, for on reading the play he threw it into the fire. But Edgar was also (and there may have been other models) at least partly based on a customs officer named Ossian Ekbohrn whom Strindberg had known earlier and who lived just outside Stockholm at Sandhamn. In an essay written in 1894 entitled *Nemesis Divina*, Strindberg described Ekbohrn as "a junior officer, brutal, uneducated, his wounded vanity thirsting for revenge on a superior". He lives with his wife, having no contact with her, isolated by "his despotism and his bullying of the islanders who hate him . . . I play the humble sympathizer who admires his broad vision of life and the universe . . . I have won his wife's heart by becoming a lightning-conductor to divert her husband's violence . . . 'For God's sake, take care!' she says to me. 'You don't realize that my husband is half-mad.' " That is precisely the situation of Alice, Edgar and Kurt in THE DANCE OF DEATH. What is curious is that Kurt, a character with whom Strindberg clearly identified himself (in an earlier draft of the play, Strindberg calls him The Stranger, *Den Okände*, the name he had given to the main and patently autobiographical character in TO DAMASCUS), should be so passive; but if Strindberg was in fact physically attracted by his sister, he may have been unwilling to portray himself as the active partner in the near-affair.

Part II he wrote some time at the end of 1900, probably in December. Emil Schering, preparing his translation of Part I for the German public, had hinted to Strindberg that he thought it too blackly pessimistic for the German

theatres to stage, and Strindberg may have written the
sequel, with its more hopeful ending (at least as regards the
younger generation) to counter this. But his notes for Part I
show that he had in mind, even at that stage, to suggest that
feuding families can be united by their children — as was to
happen with him and the Philps, for in 1907 their son
Henry married Strindberg's daughter Greta.

Despite the (one would have thought) obvious dramatic power of the two plays, especially Part I, nearly five
years elapsed before either was staged. At length, in September 1905, Part I received its première, not in Sweden
but in Cologne, and the two parts were staged together
that autumn in Berlin. During the next few years, they
were enthusiastically acclaimed; but neither play was
seen in Sweden until 1909, when Strindberg's own Intimate
Theatre presented Part I. "First and last, the Captain must
look old!" Strindberg commanded August Falck, who was
rehearsing the part. "His ugliness, age and whisky must be
visible." In his reminiscences, FEM ÅR MED STRIND-
BERG (FIVE YEARS WITH STRINDBERG) (Stockholm,
1935), Falck paints a vivid picture of the dramatist advising
his actor-director:

" 'THE DANCE OF DEATH, my boy! That's my best
play!' Strindberg often repeated . . . 'The Captain! What a
part!' And he jumped up and acted it for me. 'A refined
demon! Evil shines out of his eyes, which sometimes flash
with a glint of satanic humour. His face is bloated with
liquor and corruption, and he so relishes saying evil things
that he almost sucks them, tastes them, rolls them round
his tongue before spitting them out. He thinks of course
that he is cunning and superior, but like all stupid people
he becomes at such moments a pitiful and petulant wretch.'

"And with sweet-sour, fawning expressions, with
gestures both jaunty and pitiful, he walked around or threw
himself down into a chair. What he particularly often liked
to act was the powerful scene when Alice, with a bored
expression, plays the march *The Dance of the Boyars*,
which incites and hypnotizes the Captain to dance — wildly
and clumsily, terrifyingly. At such moments he was an

excellent actor — a great dramatic talent. His vivid imperson-
ation remains for ever in my mind's eye and echoes in my
ear."

Part I received a mixed reception from the Swedish press
when performed (as it had had when published in 1901).
August Brunius mocked it as "a pathological study of
various physical and spiritual illnesses: erotic hysteria and
sclerosis of the heart and the like. A hospital theatre would
be the most appropriate locale for THE DANCE OF
DEATH." But other critics were more perceptive, and the
play proved one of the Intimate Theatre's biggest successes,
achieving eighty-five performances. Part II, which was
presented two months later, was even more favourably
received, and reached the respectable total of sixty-five
performances. The role of Judith, the Captain's daughter,
was played by a young actress named Fanny Falkner,
who, though more than forty years Strindberg's junior,
twice became briefly engaged to him — for five days in
1909 and for a single day in 1910.

Max Reinhardt, a great Strindberg pioneer, staged a
famous production of both parts at the Deutsches Theater
in Berlin in 1912, with Paul Wegener and Gertrud Eysoldt,
and in November 1915 he brought his production to
Stockholm, where it created a sensation. He began and
ended Part I with Edgar and Alice seated on opposite sides
of the stage with their backs to the audience, staring into
space. Since then, THE DANCE OF DEATH, or at any rate
Part I, has been one of Strindberg's most frequently
performed plays, both in Sweden and abroad. London first
saw it, briefly, in 1924, when George Merritt and Sybil
Arundale acted the two parts, on separate evenings each
for a single performance at the St George's Hall under the
auspices of the Sunday Players. In 1928 Robert Loraine
gave a famous performance in the play at the Apollo
Theatre (the first Strindberg production seen in the West
End), following his success with THE FATHER the previous
year.

In 1965, Paul Scofield and Mai Zetterling acted Part I
with distinction on television, but it was not until 1966,

thirty-eight years after Loraine's triumph, that the play was revived on the London stage. That year, Glen Byam Shaw directed both parts, in a single bill, at the Old Vic for the National Theatre, with Laurence Olivier as Edgar and Geraldine McEwan as Alice. Olivier, though his appearance hardly answered Strindberg's demand for "ugliness, age and whisky", gave a predictably dynamic and scarifying performance. Another memorable interpretation of the role was that by Erich von Stroheim, in a film which he directed (in French, in Italy), in 1947; unfortunately, he had a very weak Alice. Emrys James played the Captain powerfully under John Caird's direction at the Aldwych Theatre in 1978. Less effective was Keith Hack's 1985 production at the Riverside Studios with Alan Bates and Frances de la Tour. On 17 January 1995 the Swedish actor-director Peter Stormare staged it superbly at the Almeida Theatre with John Neville and Gemma Jones.

On the occasion of the 1928 production, Charles Morgan, an outspoken champion of Strindberg in an age when most London critics regarded him as an impossible foreign crank, wrote an anonymous review in the *Times* which remains, fifty years later, a wonderfully valid assessment. "Loose, tangled and contradictory though this play often is, it leaves an astonishing, an almost unaccountable, impression of genius. To the coldly regarding eye it exhibits a crowd of faults – now of over-emphasis, now of forced movements towards a climax, now of rash inconsistency of structure; yet, as a beggar's cloak full of holes may have a kind of majestic beauty when the wind fills it, so this broken drama, having unmistakably the winds of vision in it, has beauty and dignity and power." One would add that nowadays we do not expect or particularly like a play to be what the 1920s regarded as "well-made", and that it is partly the jagged, uneven shape of Strindberg's dramas, with the characters veering sharply from mood to mood as people under the stress of violent emotion do, that makes him, more than Ibsen, the model for so many of our younger playwrights, both in England and in America.

The Dance of Death

(1900)

PART I

CHARACTERS

EDGAR, Captain at the Artillery Fortress
ALICE, his wife, an ex-actress
KURT, Quarantine Master
JENNY
THE OLD WOMAN
THE SENTRY

This translation was first performed in London on 15 June 1978 by the Royal Shakespeare Company at the Aldwych Theatre.
The cast was:

EDGAR	Emrys James
ALICE	Sheila Allen
KURT	Alan David
JENNY	Deirdra Morris
OLD WOMAN	Myrtle Moss

Designed by Mary Moore
Directed by John Caird

SCENE

The interior of a circular fortress tower, of grey stone. Upstage, two large doors with glass panes, through which can be seen the seashore, with batteries. On either side of the gateway, a window with flowers and birds. Right of the doorway, an upright piano. Downstage of this, a sewing-table with two easy chairs. Left centre, a writing-table with a telegraph apparatus; downstage, a whatnot with photographic portraits. Beside this, a chaise-longue. Against the wall, a sideboard. A ceiling lamp. On the wall by the piano hang two big laurel wreaths with ribbons, flanking a portrait of a woman in theatrical costume. By the doorway a wardrobe with uniform paraphernalia, sabres, etc. Near it, a secretaire. Left of the doorway hangs a mercury barometer.

ACT ONE

Scene 1

*It is a mild autumn evening. The doors of the fortress
stand open, and an artilleryman can be seen at his post
at the battery on the shore. He wears a helmet with
bands. Now and then his sabre glitters in the red light
of the setting sun. The sea is dark and still.*

The CAPTAIN *is seated in the armchair on the
left of the sewing-table, fingering a spent cigar. He is
in a worn undress uniform with riding-boots and spurs.
He looks tired and bored.* ALICE *is seated in the armchair on the right and is doing nothing. She looks
tired and expectant.*

CAPTAIN: Won't you play something for me?

ALICE [*indifferent, but not snappish*] : What shall I play?

CAPTAIN: What *you* wish.

ALICE: You don't like my repertoire.

CAPTAIN: Nor you mine.

ALICE [*changing the subject*]: Do you want those doors open?

CAPTAIN: If you do.

ALICE: Let them be, then. [*Pause.*] Why aren't you
smoking?

CAPTAIN: I can't stand strong tobacco nowadays.

ALICE [*almost amiably*] : Smoke something milder, then.
It's your only pleasure, you say.

CAPTAIN: Pleasure? What's that?

ALICE: Don't ask me. I'm as ignorant on the subject as
you. Don't you want your whisky yet?

CAPTAIN: I'll wait a little. What have you got for dinner?

ALICE: How should I know? Ask Christine.

CAPTAIN: Shouldn't we be getting some mackerel soon? It's autumn.

ALICE: Yes, it's autumn.

CAPTAIN: Outside and in! But, notwithstanding the chill that comes with autumn, outside and in, a grilled mackerel with a slice of lemon and a glass of white Mâcon is a thought not wholly to be despised.

ALICE: Quite the orator, aren't you?

CAPTAIN: Have we any Mâcon left in the cellar?

ALICE: I wasn't aware we'd had any cellar for the past five years.

CAPTAIN: You are always ill informed. Well, we'll have to lay some in for our silver wedding —

ALICE: You really intend to celebrate that?

CAPTAIN: Naturally.

ALICE: It would be more natural if we kept our misery private. Our twenty-five years of misery —

CAPTAIN: My dear Alice. Miserable it has been, but we have had our fun now and then. And one must enjoy the brief time one has, for after that, there is nothing.

ALICE: Is there nothing? If only we could be sure.

CAPTAIN: Nothing at all. Just a barrowload of muck to fertilize the garden.

ALICE: All this for a garden.

CAPTAIN: That's what life is. Don't blame me.

ALICE: All this. [*Pause.*] Has the post come?

CAPTAIN: Yes.

ALICE: Is the butcher's bill there?

CAPTAIN: Yes.

ALICE: How much?

CAPTAIN [*takes a piece of paper from his pocket and puts his glasses on his nose, but at once removes them*]: You read it. I can't see any more —

ALICE: What's wrong with your eyes?

CAPTAIN: Don't know.

ALICE: Age.

CAPTAIN: Oh, rubbish. Me!

ALICE: Well, not me.

CAPTAIN: Hm!

ALICE [*looks at the bill*]: Can you pay this?

CAPTAIN: Yes. But not now.

ALICE: Later. In a year, when you're retired on a small pension. And that'll be too late. And you'll be ill again —

CAPTAIN: Ill? I've never been ill. Just out of sorts, once. I'll live for twenty years.

ALICE: The Doctor thought otherwise.

CAPTAIN: The Doctor!

ALICE: Well, who else should know?

CAPTAIN: There's nothing wrong with me and there never has been. And never will be. I'll die with my boots on, as an old soldier should.

ALICE: Talking of the Doctor, you know he's giving a party this evening.

CAPTAIN [*disturbed*]: Well, so what? We aren't invited because we don't mix with them, and we don't mix with them because I despise them both. They're trash.

ALICE: You say that of everyone.

CAPTAIN: Because everyone is trash.

ALICE: Except you.

CAPTAIN: Yes, because I have behaved like a gentleman
whatever life has thrown at me. That is why I am not
trash.

    Pause.

ALICE: Do you want to play cards?

CAPTAIN: Why not?

ALICE [*takes out a pack of cards from the drawer of the
sewing-table and begins to shuffle it*]: You know he's got
the regimental band. For a private party!

CAPTAIN [*angry*]: That's because he sneaks off to town
with the Colonel! Dirty little creeper. If I'd chosen to do
that —

ALICE [*deals*]: I used to be friends with Gerda. But she
cheated me —

CAPTAIN: They're all cheats. [*Peers at the trump marker.*]
What are trumps?

ALICE: Put your glasses on.

CAPTAIN: They won't help. Come on.

ALICE: Spades are trumps.

CAPTAIN [*displeased*]: Spades?

ALICE [*plays a card*]: Anyway, it's not just them. The new
officers' wives don't want anything to do with us either.

CAPTAIN [*plays and takes the trick*]: What does that
matter? We never give parties, so we won't notice. I can
manage alone. I always have. ·

ALICE: So have I. But the children. The children grow up
without knowing anyone.

CAPTAIN: They'll have to find their own friends, in town. My trick! Have you any trumps left?

ALICE: I've got one. That's mine!

CAPTAIN: Six and eight make fifteen —

ALICE: Fourteen, fourteen.

CAPTAIN: Six and eight makes fourteen points to me. I think I've forgotten how to count. And two makes sixteen. [*Yawns.*] Your deal.

ALICE: You're tired.

CAPTAIN [*deals*]: Not at all.

ALICE [*listens*]: You can hear the music from here. [*Pause*] Do you think Kurt's been invited?

CAPTAIN: He came this morning, so he's had time to get his tails out, though not to visit us.

ALICE: Quarantine Master? Is there to be a quarantine here?

CAPTAIN: Yes.

ALICE: I mean he is my cousin, and we once shared the same name —

CAPTAIN: That was no honour.

ALICE: Look — ! [*Sharply.*] You forget about my family and I'll forget about yours.

CAPTAIN: Now, now! Are we going to start again?

ALICE: Does the Quarantine Master have to be a doctor?

CAPTAIN: No. He's just a kind of administrator and book-keeper. And Kurt's never been either.

ALICE: He's had a hard life —

CAPTAIN: He cost me money. And when he left his wife and children, he lost what honour he had.

ALICE: There's no need to be so harsh, Edgar.

CAPTAIN: Well, it's true. Remember what happened later in America? Well! I can't say I miss him. But he was a nice lad and I liked arguing with him.

ALICE: Because he always gave in.

CAPTAIN [*haughtily*]: Gave in, gave in, at least he was a man one could talk to. On this island there isn't anyone who understands what I say. It's a community of imbeciles —

ALICE: It's strange that Kurt should come just at the time of our silver wedding — whether we celebrate it or not —

CAPTAIN: Why is it strange? Oh, I see — yes, it was he who brought us together. Married you off, was the phrase they used.

ALICE: Well, he did, didn't he?

CAPTAIN: Oh, yes! He got some idea into his head — well, you should know best.

ALICE: It was just a whim —

CAPTAIN: Which we have had to suffer for. Not he.

ALICE: Yes. Think if I'd stayed in the theatre. All my friends are stars now.

CAPTAIN [*gets up*]: Oh, we're back there, are we? I'll have a whisky. [*Goes to the sideboard and pours a whisky and soda, which he drinks standing.*] We ought to have a rail to rest our feet on. Then we could dream we were in Copenhagen, at the American Bar.

ALICE: We must have one made, if it'll remind us of Copenhagen. Those were our happiest days, in spite of everything.

CAPTAIN [*drinks greedily*]: Yes! Do you remember Nimb's charlotte russe? [*Smacks his lips.*]

ALICE: No. But I remember the concerts at Tivoli.

CAPTAIN: You have such refined taste, my dear.

ALICE: You should be proud, at having a wife with taste —

CAPTAIN: I am.

ALICE: When you need to boast about her —

CAPTAIN [drinks]: They must be dancing at the Doctor's now. I can hear the trombones — [hums in waltz rhythm] — oompapa, oompapa —

ALICE: I can hear the Alcazar waltz. Yes — it's a long time since I danced a waltz —

CAPTAIN: Could you still manage it?

ALICE: Still?

CAPTAIN: We-ell? You're done with dancing, aren't you, like me?

ALICE: I'm ten years younger than you.

CAPTAIN: Then we are the same age, since the lady is always ten years younger.

ALICE: Stuff! You're an old man. I'm in my prime.

CAPTAIN: But of course! You can be delightful — to other men, when you try.

ALICE: Can we light the lamp now?

CAPTAIN: Why not?

ALICE: Ring, then.

> The CAPTAIN walks heavily to the desk and rings the bell. JENNY enters right.

CAPTAIN: Jenny, would you mind lighting the lamp, please?

ALICE [sharply]: Light the lamp!

JENNY: Very good, madam.

> She lights the ceiling lamp. The CAPTAIN watches her.

ALICE [*curtly*] : Have you dried the glass properly?

JENNY: Yes, all it needs.

ALICE: How dare you answer like that?

CAPTAIN: Alice — please —

ALICE [*to* JENNY] : Get out! I'd better light the lamp
   myself.

JENNY: Yes, I think you had. [*Walks towards door.*]

ALICE [*gets up*] : Go!

JENNY [*pauses*] : I wonder what you'd say if I did?
      ALICE *is silent.* JENNY *goes. The* CAPTAIN *walks*
      over and lights the lamp.

ALICE [*uneasily*] : Do you think she will go?

CAPTAIN: Wouldn't surprise me. We'll be in a hole if she
   does.

ALICE: It's your fault. You spoil them.

CAPTAIN: Nonsense. They're always polite to me.

ALICE: Because you cringe to them. You cringe to all
   subordinates, because you're a bully with a slave's mentality.

CAPTAIN: Very clever.

ALICE: Yes, you cringe to your men and your junior
   officers, but you can't come to terms with your equals and
   your superiors.

CAPTAIN: Pah!

ALICE: You're like all bullies. Do you think she'll leave?

CAPTAIN: Yes, if you don't go and talk nicely to her.

ALICE: I?

CAPTAIN: If I did, you'd say I was flirting with the
   servants.

ALICE: Think if she does go! Then I'll have to do all the
   work again, and ruin my hands.

CAPTAIN: I can imagine worse things. But if Jenny goes, Christine will go, and then we shan't get another servant to come to this island. The ferry pilot frightens off every girl who comes to apply, and if he forgets to, my sentries will.

ALICE: Yes, your sentries. Whom I have to feed in my kitchen, and whom you haven't the courage to order out —

CAPTAIN: If I did, they'd go too, and we'd be left without a garrison.

ALICE: But it's ruining us.

CAPTAIN: Which is why the mess committee intend to apply to His Majesty for a subsistence allowance —

ALICE: For us?

CAPTAIN: No, for the sentries.

ALICE [laughs]: You're crazy.

CAPTAIN: Yes, laugh a little for me. We need some mirth.

ALICE: I'll soon have forgotten how to laugh.

CAPTAIN [lights his cigar]: One must never forget that. It's a bit of a bore, though.

ALICE: It certainly isn't funny. Do you want to go on playing?

CAPTAIN: No, it tires me.

    Pause.

ALICE: You know, it does annoy me that my cousin, our new Quarantine Master, should pay his respects to our enemies before he comes and sees us.

CAPTAIN: Oh, why bother about that?

ALICE: Well, did you see in the paper that the list of arrivals described him as "of independent means"? That means he must have come into money.

CAPTAIN: Independent means? Indeed! A rich relation! First we've ever had in this family.

ALICE: In your family. We've had plenty of rich ones in mine.

CAPTAIN: He's got hold of some money, so he's giving himself airs. But I know how to play him. He won't get a look at my cards.

The telegraph apparatus begins to click.

ALICE: Who's that?

CAPTAIN [*stands still*] : Quiet a moment, please!

ALICE: Well, go and see what it says.

CAPTAIN: I can hear. I hear what they're saying. It's the children! [*Goes to the apparatus and taps out a reply. The apparatus taps back. The* CAPTAIN *answers.*]

ALICE: Well?

CAPTAIN: Wait a moment. [*Taps the "stop" signal.*] It's the children. Judith is ill again. She's staying away from school.

ALICE: Again! What else did they say?

CAPTAIN: Money, of course.

ALICE: Why does Judith have to be in such a hurry? If she took her exams next year it'd be soon enough.

CAPTAIN: You tell her that and see what good it does.

ALICE: You should tell her.

CAPTAIN: How many times haven't I? You should know that children do as they please.

ALICE: In this house, anyway. [*The* CAPTAIN *yawns.*] Must you yawn in your wife's presence?

CAPTAIN: What else is there to do? Haven't you noticed

that every day we say the same things? When just now you said your inevitable "In this house, anyway", I should have replied as usual "It's not just *my* house". But since I've given that answer five hundred times already, I merely yawned. My yawn could mean "I can't be bothered to reply", or "You are right, my angel", or "For God's sake let's stop".

ALICE: You're being really charming tonight.

CAPTAIN: Won't it be time for dinner soon?

ALICE: Do you know the doctor has ordered supper from the Grand Hotel? On the mainland.

CAPTAIN: No? Then they'll be having grouse. There's no finer bird than grouse. But one mustn't roast it in lard.

ALICE: Ugh! Must you talk about food?

CAPTAIN: You prefer wine? I wonder what those Philistines will drink with grouse.

ALICE: Shall I play for you?

CAPTAIN [*sits at his desk*]: The last resort! Yes, as long as we don't have any of your funeral marches and jeremiads. There's no need to underline the obvious. I can always fill in the words. "Hear how miserable I am! Miaow, miaow! Hear what a frightful husband I have! Brum, brum, brum! Oh, if only he would die!" Kettledrums, fanfares! And we end with the Alcazar waltz and a champagne gallop! Talking of champagne, we have two bottles left. Shall we open them and pretend we've guests?

ALICE: No, we won't. They're mine. I bought them myself.

CAPTAIN: Always careful with the purse-strings, aren't you?

ALICE: And you're always mean, to your wife at any rate.

CAPTAIN: Then I've no further ideas. Shall I dance for you?

ALICE: No, thank you. You're too old to dance.

CAPTAIN: You should have a female companion to live with you.

ALICE: Thank you. You should have a male.

CAPTAIN: Thank you. That was tried, and the result was mutual dissatisfaction. But interesting, as an experiment — I mean, that as soon as a stranger entered the house, you and I became so happy — to begin with —

ALICE: But afterwards!

CAPTAIN: Yes, let's not talk of that.

There is a knock on the door, left.

ALICE: Who can that be at this hour?

CAPTAIN: Jenny doesn't usually knock.

ALICE: Go and open it, and don't shout "Come in!" as though you were in an office.

CAPTAIN [*goes towards the door*]: You don't like anything associated with work, do you?

Another knock.

ALICE: Well, open it!

CAPTAIN [*opens it and is handed a visiting card*]: It's Christine. Has Jenny left? [*Inaudible reply.*] [*To* ALICE]: Jenny's left.

ALICE: I'll have to be a housemaid again, then.

CAPTAIN: And I a valet.

ALICE: Can't we use one of the men from the kitchen?

CAPTAIN: One can't do that nowadays.

ALICE: That card can't have been Jenny's, surely?

CAPTAIN [*looks at the card through his glasses, then hands it to* ALICE]: You read it. I can't.

ALICE [*reads*]: Kurt! It's Kurt! Go out and greet him!

CAPTAIN [*exits left*]: Kurt! Well, how nice!

> ALICE *arranges her hair and seems to become alive.*
> *The* CAPTAIN *enters left with* KURT.

CAPTAIN: Well here he is, the renegade! Welcome, my dear chap. Good to see you.

ALICE [*to* KURT]: Welcome to my house, Kurt.

KURT: Thank you. It's been a long time.

CAPTAIN: What is it, fifteen years? And we've grown old —

ALICE: Oh, Kurt hasn't changed, I don't think.

CAPTAIN: Sit down, sit down! Now, first of all, what's your programme? Are you booked for dinner tonight?

KURT: I've been invited to the Doctor's, but I haven't promised to come.

ALICE: Then you'll stay with us?

KURT: That would seem the most natural thing, since you are my relatives. But the Doctor is my boss, and it might be awkward later —

CAPTAIN: What nonsense! I've never been scared of my bosses —

KURT: I didn't say I was scared. It just might be awkward.

CAPTAIN: On this island, I'm the master. You get behind me and no one will dare to harm you.

ALICE: Be quiet now, Edgar. [*Takes* KURT's *hand.*] Never mind about bosses and masters — you stay here with us. People will think that natural and correct.

KURT: Very well, then. You certainly make me feel welcome here.

CAPTAIN: Why shouldn't you be welcome? We've no quarrel, have we? [KURT *cannot conceal a certain embarrassment.*] What could there be? You were a bit thoughtless once, but you were young and I've forgotten it. I don't bear grudges.

ALICE *is embarrassed. They all sit at the sewing-table.*

ALICE: Well, you've been out in the wide world.

KURT: Yes. And now I'm back here with both of you —

CAPTAIN: Whom you married off twenty-five years ago.

KURT: I didn't quite do that, but never mind. It's good to see you're still together after twenty-five years —

CAPTAIN: Yes, we've managed. We've had our ups and downs, but as you say, we're still together. And Alice has no cause to complain; everything's gone fine, money has been pouring in. Perhaps you don't know that I am a famous author — in the educational field —

KURT: Oh, yes, I remember when we last saw each other, you'd published a rifle instruction handbook that had gone well. Do they still use it in the army schools —?

CAPTAIN: It's still in print, and it's still the best, though they've tried to replace it with an inferior one — which gets read, but is quite worthless.

Painful silence.

KURT: You've been abroad, I hear?

ALICE: Yes, we've been to Copenhagen. Five times, imagine!

CAPTAIN: Yes! You see, when I took Alice out of the theatre —

ALICE: Took? You?

CAPTAIN: Yes, I took you as a wife should be taken —

ALICE: How dashing of you.

CAPTAIN: But since it was subsequently shoved down my throat that I had cut short her brilliant career — hm! — I had to make up for this by promising to take my wife to Copenhagen — and that promise I have kept — like a gentleman! Five times we have been there! Five. [*Counts the fingers on his left hand.*] Have you been in Copenhagen?

KURT [*smiles*] : No. I've mostly been in America.

CAPTAIN: America? That must be a frightful country, nothing but gangsters.

KURT [*embarrassed*] : Well, it isn't Copenhagen.

ALICE: Have you — heard anything — from your children?

KURT: No.

ALICE: Forgive me, Kurt dear, but it was rather thoughtless of you to leave them like you did —

KURT: I didn't leave them. The court awarded custody to their mother —

CAPTAIN: Let's not discuss that now. I think you were well out of that mess.

KURT [*to* ALICE] : How are your children?

ALICE: Oh, fine, thank you. They're at school in town. They're almost grown up.

CAPTAIN: Yes, they're clever kids. The boy's got a brilliant brain. Brilliant. He's going onto the General Staff —

ALICE: If they take him.

CAPTAIN: If? He'll be Minister of Defence.

KURT: Changing the subject — there's going to be a quarantine here — bubonic plague, cholera and all that. As you know, I'll be working under the Doctor. What kind of a chap is he?

CAPTAIN: Chap? He isn't a chap. He's an ignorant rogue.

KURT [*to* ALICE] : How very unpleasant for me!

ALICE: He's not as bad as Edgar makes out, but I can't say I like him —

CAPTAIN: He's a rogue! And so are the others, the excise officer, the postmaster, the telephone woman, the chemist, the pilot, the — what does he call himself? — alderman — they're all a pack of rogues, which is why I have nothing to do with them.

KURT: Are you at loggerheads with all of them?

CAPTAIN: All!

ALICE: Yes, it's true. One really can't associate with such people.

CAPTAIN: Every bullying little bureaucrat in the country seems to have been sent here.

ALICE [sarcastically]: Every one!

CAPTAIN [genially]: Hm! Is that a reference to me? I am no bully, at any rate not in my own house.

ALICE: I'd like to see you try.

CAPTAIN [to KURT]: You mustn't listen to what she says. I'm a very good husband, and my old lady's the best wife in the world.

ALICE: Kurt, would you like a drink?

KURT: Thank you, not now.

CAPTAIN: Have you become a — ?

KURT: I just don't drink much.

CAPTAIN: America?

KURT: Yes.

CAPTAIN: I don't go with moderation. A man ought to be able to hold his drink.

KURT: These neighbours of yours. In my job I shall have to meet them all — and it'll be tricky, because even if one doesn't want to get involved, one gets involved in other people's intrigues.

ALICE: You go and meet them. You'll always come back to us. We're your true friends.

KURT: Isn't it horrible to sit alone surrounded by enemies, like you do?

ALICE: It isn't fun.

CAPTAIN: It isn't at all horrible! I've had nothing but enemies all my life, and they've helped me on my way, not harmed me. And when I have to die, I shall be able to say that I owe nobody anything and have never received anything gratis. Every stick I own I've had to fight for.

ALICE: Yes, Edgar's path has not been paved with roses —

CAPTAIN: With thorns, stones, flints — I've had to trust in my own strength. Same with you?

KURT [simply]: I learned the inadequacy of that ten years ago.

CAPTAIN: Then you're pathetic.

ALICE: Edgar!

CAPTAIN: Yes, he's pathetic if he doesn't trust in his own strength. It's true that when the mechanism runs down you're a barrowload of shit to scatter over the garden, but as long as the cogs go round you must kick and fight, with your fists and your feet. As long as the threads hold together. That's my philosophy.

KURT [smiles]: You're fun to listen to.

CAPTAIN: But don't you think I'm right?

KURT: No, I don't.

CAPTAIN: Well, it's the truth, anyway.

> During the preceding dialogue the wind has risen, and now one of the doors upstage bangs to.

CAPTAIN [rises]: The wind's getting up. I felt it would. [Goes over, shuts the door and taps the barometer.]

ALICE [to KURT]: You'll stay with us for supper?

KURT: Thank you, if I may.

ALICE: But it'll be very simple. Our maid has left.

KURT: That'll suit me.

ALICE: Dear Kurt, you're so unpretentious.

CAPTAIN [by the barometer]: Extraordinary how the barometer's fallen. I felt it!

ALICE [whispers to KURT]: He's so nervous.

CAPTAIN: We ought to eat soon.

ALICE [gets up]: I'll go and see to it. You two sit down and philosophize. [Whispers to KURT.] Don't contradict him or he'll lose his temper. And don't ask why he never became a major.

    KURT nods. ALICE goes right.

CAPTAIN [sits at sewing-table with KURT]: Cook us something worth eating, now, old lady.

ALICE: Give me some money, and I will.

CAPTAIN: Always money!

    ALICE exits.

CAPTAIN [to KURT]: Money, money, money! I spend the whole day opening my purse, so that I've finally come to believe I am a purse! Do you know that feeling?

KURT: Oh, yes. The only difference was, I used to think I was a wallet.

CAPTAIN [laughs]: You've sucked that lemon too? These women! [Laughs again.] And you caught a real tartar.

KURT [patiently]: Let's forget that, now.

CAPTAIN: She was a proper pearl. Whereas mine's a good woman, for all her faults. She's all right. For all her faults.

KURT [smiles good-humouredly]: For all her faults!

CAPTAIN: Don't laugh, damn you.

KURT [*as before*] : For all her faults.

CAPTAIN: Yes, she's been a faithful wife, and an excellent mother — first-rate — it's just that — [*Glances at door*] — She's got a devilish temper. Do you know, there have been moments when I've cursed you for saddling me with her?

KURT [*amiably*] : But I didn't. Look here, old chap —

CAPTAIN: Oh, come on. You're talking rubbish, you forget things you don't want to remember. Oh, don't take it amiss, I'm used to ordering people about and swearing at them. You know me, I know you won't take offence.

KURT: Of course not. But I didn't get you your wife. Quite the opposite.

CAPTAIN [*in full spate, regardless*] : Life's odd though, don't you think?

KURT: I suppose it is.

CAPTAIN: And getting old. It isn't nice, but it's interesting. Oh, I'm no age, but I'm beginning to feel it. All one's acquaintances die off, and one feels so alone.

KURT: Lucky the man who has a wife to grow old with.

CAPTAIN: Lucky? Yes, I suppose you're right — one's children leave one too. You shouldn't have left yours.

KURT: But I didn't. They were taken from me —

CAPTAIN: Now you mustn't get angry when I mention it.

KURT: But it didn't happen —

CAPTAIN: Well, whether it did or not, it's forgotten now. But you're on your own!

KURT: One can get used to anything, my dear fellow.

CAPTAIN: Can one? Can one get used to — to being quite alone?

KURT: Well, look at me.

CAPTAIN: What have you been doing these fifteen years?

KURT: What a question! I mean, fifteen years —

CAPTAIN: They say you've come into money, and are rich.

KURT: I wouldn't say rich —

CAPTAIN: I'm not trying to touch you —

KURT: If you were, I'd gladly —

CAPTAIN: Thank you very much, but I have money. You see — [*looks at the door*] — there must be no want in this house. The day I had no money — she would leave me.

KURT: Oh, no —

CAPTAIN: No? I know it! Would you believe it, she always remarks on it when I'm out of money, just for the pleasure of impressing it on me that I don't look after my family.

KURT: But you have a big income, I remember your saying.

CAPTAIN: Certainly I have a big income. But it isn't big enough.

KURT: Then it can't be big, in the usual sense —

CAPTAIN: Life is strange and so are we.

The telegraph starts tapping.

KURT: What is that?

CAPTAIN: Only a time-signal.

KURT: Haven't you a telephone?

CAPTAIN: Yes, in the kitchen. But we use the telegraph because the telephone-operators repeat everything we say.

KURT: It must be dreadful for you all, living out here.

CAPTAIN: It's perfectly gruesome. All life is gruesome. Kurt, you believe in an after-life. Do you suppose we shall find peace — afterwards?

KURT: I suppose there'll be storms and strife there too.

CAPTAIN: There too. If there is any "there". Better if there is nothing.

KURT: Can you be sure that annihilation would happen without pain?

CAPTAIN: I shall die snap! without pain.

KURT: You're sure of that?

CAPTAIN: Yes. I know it.

KURT: You don't seem content with your existence?

CAPTAIN [*sighs*]: Content? The day I'm allowed to die, I shall be content.

KURT: You can't be sure of that. But tell me, what do you do in this house? What happens here? The walls smell of poison — one feels ill the moment one enters. I'd like to leave, if I hadn't promised Alice to stay. There are corpses under the floorboards; there's such hatred here, it's difficult to breathe.

The CAPTAIN *slumps in his chair and stares vacantly ahead of him.*

KURT: What's the matter? Edgar! [*The* CAPTAIN *remains motionless.* KURT *slaps him on the shoulder.*] Edgar!

CAPTAIN [*comes to himself*]: Did you say something? [*Looks around.*] I thought it was Alice. Oh, it's you? Look, I — [*Becomes torpid again.*]

KURT: This is horrible! [*Goes to the door right, and opens it.*] Alice!

ALICE [*enters, wearing a kitchen apron*]: What is it?

KURT: I don't know. Look at him!

ALICE [*calmly*]: He goes off like that sometimes. I'll play some music, then he'll wake up.

KURT: No, don't do that. Let me look at him. Can he hear? Can he see?

ALICE: Now he can neither hear nor see.

KURT: And you can say that so calmly! Alice, what is going on in this house?

ALICE: Ask that thing.

KURT: That thing? He is your husband!

ALICE: To me he is a stranger, as much a stranger as he was twenty-five years ago. I know nothing about that man — except that —

KURT: Hush! He can hear you.

ALICE: He can hear nothing.

A bugle sounds outside.

CAPTAIN [*jumps up, takes his sabre and military cap*]: Excuse me! I must just inspect the sentries. [*Goes out through rear doors.*]

KURT: Is he ill?

ALICE: I don't know.

KURT: Is he out of his mind?

ALICE: I don't know.

KURT: Does he drink?

ALICE: Not as much as he boasts he does.

KURT: Sit down and tell me. But calmly, and the truth.

ALICE [*sits*]: What shall I say? That I have sat in this tower for a lifetime, a prisoner, kept from life by a man I have always hated, and whom I now hate so boundlessly that the day he died I would laugh for joy!

KURT: Why haven't you parted?

ALICE: You may well ask. We parted twice when we were engaged, we've tried to part ever since, every day — but we are welded together, and can't prise ourselves loose. Once we did part — in here, without leaving the house.

Once in five years! Now only death can part us. We know that, and so we await him as a liberator.

KURT: Why are you so alone, the two of you?

ALICE: Because he isolates me. First he rooted out all my brothers and sisters from the house — that's the phrase he used, rooted out. Then my woman friends, and others —

KURT: But *his* relatives? Did you root them out?

ALICE: Yes. They would have robbed me of my life, once they had robbed me of my honour. In the end I had to maintain contact with the outside world through that telegraph, because the telephone-operators eavesdropped on our conversations. I taught myself to use the telegraph, though he doesn't know that. You mustn't tell him, or he'll kill me.

KURT: Horrible! Horrible! But why does he blame me for your marriage? You remember how it was. Edgar and I were friends. He fell in love with you as soon as he saw you, came to me and begged me to act as intermediary. I refused, and — my dear Alice, I knew how cruel and tyrannical you could be — so I warned him, and when he persisted, I told him to get your brother to plead his cause to you.

ALICE: I believe you. But he's been lying to himself about it all these years, and you'll never be able to persuade him otherwise.

KURT: Well, let him blame me, if it'll make him feel easier.

ALICE: That's too much to ask —

KURT: Oh, I'm used to it. But what does hurt me is his saying that I abandoned my children. That's quite untrue —

ALICE: Oh, that's his way. He says what he thinks, and then believes it. But he seems fond of you, mostly because you don't contradict him. Do try to go along with us. I think you came here at a lucky moment for us. Really, it's an act of providence. Kurt, you must help us. We're the most miserable couple on earth. [*Weeps.*]

KURT: I've seen one marriage at close quarters — and that was frightening. But this is almost worse.

ALICE: You think so?

KURT: Yes.

ALICE: Whose fault is it?

KURT: Alice! The moment you stop asking whose fault it is, things will be easier. Try to accept it as a fact, as a trial, which must be endured —

ALICE: I can't! It's too much. [*Gets up.*] It's so hopeless.

KURT: Unhappy people! Do you know why you hate each other?

ALICE: No. It's got no logic — no grounds, no purpose — but no end. Can you imagine what he most fears from death? He fears that I shall re-marry!

KURT: Then he does love you.

ALICE: So it seems. But that doesn't prevent him hating me.

KURT [*as though to himself*]: It is what men call the hatred of love, and is born in hell. Does he like you to play for him?

ALICE: Yes, but only ugly tunes. This frightful *March of the Boyars*. When he hears that he becomes possessed and wants to dance.

KURT: Does *he* dance?

ALICE: Yes. He has these whims.

KURT: One thing — forgive my asking. Where are the children?

ALICE: Two of them died, did you know?

KURT: You've been through that too?

ALICE: What haven't I been through?

KURT: But the other two?

ALICE: They're in town. They couldn't live at home. He turned them against me —

KURT: And you turned them against him.

ALICE: Of course. And then we had political intrigues, canvassing, bribes — in the end we sent the children away so as not to destroy them. What should have been our bond divided us; what should have been a blessing became a curse. Sometimes I think we belong to a race that is cursed.

KURT: Well, yes, we are, Since we first sinned —

ALICE [with a spiteful glance, sharply]: What do you mean?

KURT: Adam and Eve.

ALICE: Oh. I thought you meant something else.

Embarrassed silence.

ALICE [clasps her hands]: Kurt! We're cousins, you've been my friend since childhood. I haven't always treated you as I should. But now I am punished, and you have your revenge on me.

KURT: Revenge! I have taken no revenge. Alice!

ALICE: Do you remember one Sunday, when you were engaged? I'd invited you to dinner.

KURT: Alice!

ALICE: I must talk — please. When you arrived we were out and you had to go away —

KURT: You'd been invited out yourselves. What does that matter now?

ALICE: Kurt! When, just now, I invited you to dine with

us, I thought there was something in the larder. [*Hides her face in her hands.*] And there's nothing, not even a piece of bread — [*Weeps.*]

KURT: Poor, poor Alice.

ALICE: But when *he* comes back and wants something to eat and there isn't anything, he'll get angry. You've never seen him angry. Oh, God, this humiliation!

KURT: Why not let me go out and get something?

ALICE: There *is* nothing to get on this island.

KURT: Look — I couldn't care less, but for his sake and yours — let me think up something, something . . . We must laugh it off as a joke. When he comes back, I'll suggest we have a drink, then I'll think up something — get him in a good humour, play some game with him, it doesn't matter what — You sit down at the piano and be ready.

ALICE: Look at my hands. What are they to play with? I have to scour the pots and dry the glasses, lay the fires, clean the house —

KURT: But you have two servants.

ALICE: We have to say we have, because he's an officer — but they're always leaving, so that sometimes we have none at all — most of the time. How shall I get out of this business about supper? Oh, if only the house would burn down — !

KURT: Alice! Don't say such things.

ALICE: Or the sea would rise and swallow us up!

KURT: No, no, no! I can't listen to you!

ALICE: What will he say, what will he say? Don't go, Kurt, don't leave me.

KURT: No, Alice. I won't go.

ALICE: Yes, but when you have gone —

KURT: Has he struck you?

ALICE: Me? Oh, no — then he knows I would go. One must cling to a little pride.

Offstage shouts of : "Halt! Who goes there?" "Friend."

KURT [*gets up*]: Is that him?

ALICE [*frightened*]: Yes.

Pause.

KURT: What on earth shall we do?

ALICE: I don't know, I don't know.

CAPTAIN [*enters upstage, in a good humour*]: There! Now I'm free. Well, Kurt, now she's had the chance to beat her breast. Makes your heart bleed, doesn't it?

KURT: What's the weather like out there?

CAPTAIN: There's a storm blowing up. [*Jovially, opening one of the doors slightly.*] Baron Bluebeard with the maiden in his tower! And outside stalks the sentry with drawn sabre, to guard the fair virgin. Along come her brothers, but there goes the sentry, see! Left, right! He's a good watchdog. Look at him! Tum-titti, tum-tum, tum-titti-tum! Shall we dance the sword dance? Kurt should see that.

KURT: No, let's have the *March of the Boyars* instead.

CAPTAIN: You know that? Alice, sit down in your apron and play. Play, I say!

She goes unwillingly to the piano. The CAPTAIN *pinches her arm.*

CAPTAIN [*to* ALICE]: You've been telling lies about me.

ALICE: I?

The CAPTAIN *turns away.* ALICE *plays the* March of the Boyars. *The* CAPTAIN *performs a Hungarian dance behind the desk, clashing his spurs. Suddenly*

he slumps to the floor, unnoticed by KURT *and*
ALICE. *She plays the piece to its conclusion.*

ALICE [*without turning her head*] : Shall we give an encore?

Silence. She turns and sees the CAPTAIN *lying
senseless, hidden from the audience by the desk.*

ALICE: Blessed Jesus!

*She stands with her arms crossed over her breasts, and
gives a sigh as of thankfulness and relief.*

KURT [*turns and runs over to the* CAPTAIN] : What's
happened? What is it?

ALICE [*tensely*] : Is he dead?

KURT: I don't know. Help me.

ALICE [*stays motionless*] : I can't touch him. Is he dead?

KURT: No. He is alive.

ALICE *sighs. The* CAPTAIN *gets up.* KURT *helps
him to a chair.*

CAPTAIN: What has happened? [*Silence.*] What has
happened?

KURT: You fell.

CAPTAIN: Did something happen?

KURT: You fell on the floor. Is something the matter?

CAPTAIN: With me? Nothing at all. Not that I'm aware of.
What are you staring at?

KURT: You're ill.

CAPTAIN: Rubbish. Go on playing, Alice. Ah! There it is
again! [*Clutches his head.*]

ALICE: There, you see. You are ill.

CAPTAIN: Don't shout. I'm just a bit dizzy.

KURT: We must get the Doctor. I'll go and telephone.

CAPTAIN: I don't want any doctor.

KURT: You must. We must get him, for our sake. Otherwise it'll be our responsibility.

CAPTAIN: If he comes, I'll kick him out. I'll put a bullet in him. Ah! There it is again! [*Clutches his head.*]

KURT [*goes to door, right*]: I'll go and telephone.

    He goes. ALICE *takes off her apron.*

CAPTAIN: Will you give me a glass of water?

ALICE: I suppose I must. [*Gives it to him.*]

CAPTAIN: Charming!

ALICE: Are you ill?

CAPTAIN: Forgive me for not being well.

ALICE: Do you want to nurse yourself, then?

CAPTAIN: You don't want to nurse me, do you?

ALICE: What do you think?

CAPTAIN: The moment is come for which you have waited so long.

ALICE: Yes. And which you thought would never come.

CAPTAIN: Don't be angry with me.

KURT [*enters right*]: It's monstrous — !

ALICE: What did he say?

KURT: He rang off, just like that.

ALICE [*to* CAPTAIN]: Well. Now you see the result of your arrogance.

CAPTAIN: I think I'm — feeling worse. Try to get a doctor from town.

ALICE [*goes to the telegraph*]: I'll have to telegraph, then.

CAPTAIN [*half-rises, amazed*]: Can — you — telegraph?

ALICE [*starts to work the machine*]: Yes. I can.

CAPTAIN: I see. Well, do it then. Damned liar she is. [*To* KURT.] Come and sit beside me. [KURT *does so.*] Hold my hand. I'm sitting and falling. Can you imagine that? Down — down — strange!

KURT: Have you had these attacks before?

CAPTAIN: Never!

KURT: While you're waiting for a reply from town, I'll go to the Doctor and talk to him. He's attended you before?

CAPTAIN: He has.

KURT: Then he knows your background. [*Goes towards exit, left.*]

ALICE: I'll get a reply soon. Thank you, Kurt. But come back quickly.

KURT: As quickly as I can. [*Exit.*]

CAPTAIN: He's a good fellow, Kurt. How he's changed!

ALICE: Yes, and for the better. I pity him, though, getting mixed up with us just now.

CAPTAIN: On our silver jubilee! I wonder how things are with him really? Did you notice, he didn't want to talk about that?

ALICE: Yes, I noticed. Though I don't think anyone asked him.

CAPTAIN: What a life he's had. And us! I wonder if everyone's life is like this?

ALICE: Perhaps. Though they don't talk about it, like we do.

CAPTAIN: Sometimes I have thought that misery attracts misery, and that happy people somehow avoid disaster. Which is why we shall never know anything but misery.

ALICE: Have you known any happy people?

CAPTAIN: Let me think. No. Yes. The Ekmarks.

ALICE: How can you say that? She had that operation
last year —

CAPTAIN: That's true. Well, I don't know. Yes, the Kraffts.

ALICE: Oh, yes! They all lived an idyllic existence — rich,
respected, nice children, good marriages — till the parents
were fifty. Then their cousin comes along, turns out to be
a criminal, gets sent to prison, and that was the end of
their happiness. Their name was plastered across every
newspaper, and they didn't dare show their face in the
street. The children had to be taken away from school . . .
Dear God!

CAPTAIN: I wonder what I've got.

ALICE: What do you think it is?

CAPTAIN: My heart, or my head. It's as though my soul
wanted to fly out of my body and disappear in a cloud
of smoke.

ALICE: Do you feel like some food?

CAPTAIN: Yes. What have we got for supper?

ALICE [walks uneasily across the room]: I'll ask Jenny.

CAPTAIN: She's left.

ALICE: Oh, yes, of course.

CAPTAIN: Ring for Christine to bring me some fresh
water.

ALICE [rings the bell]: Imagine — ! [Rings again.] She
doesn't hear.

CAPTAIN: Go outside and see if — imagine if she's left
too!

ALICE [goes over to door left and opens it]: What's this?
Her trunk's standing packed in the corridor.

CAPTAIN: Then she has left.

ALICE: This is hell! [*Begins to weep, falls to her knees and lays her head against a chair, sobbing.*]

CAPTAIN: And all at once! And of course Kurt has to come and see the mess we're in. Just to add an extra humiliation. He has to come, just now.

ALICE: Do you know what I think? I think he's gone too. And won't come back.

CAPTAIN: I can believe that of him.

ALICE: Yes. We are cursed —

CAPTAIN: What's that?

ALICE: Don't you see how everyone shuns us?

CAPTAIN: Let them! [*The telegraph starts tapping.*] There's your answer. Quiet, I'm listening ... "No one has time." They're avoiding us. The scum!

ALICE: That's the result of abusing your doctors. And neglecting to pay them.

CAPTAIN: That's not true —

ALICE: Even when you could, you wouldn't pay them, because you despised their work, just as you have despised my work and everyone else's. Now they won't come. And the telephone's cut off, because you didn't think that worth having either. Nothing's worth anything to you except your rifles and cannons.

CAPTAIN: Don't stand there talking rubbish.

ALICE: Everything comes back. Life is a circle.

CAPTAIN: Superstitious nonsense! An old wives' tale.

ALICE: You'll see. Do you know we owe Christine six months' salary?

CAPTAIN: Well, she's stolen that much.

ALICE: But I've had to borrow money from her.

CAPTAIN: I can believe that of you.

ALICE: How ungrateful you are! You know I only did it so that the children could visit us.

CAPTAIN: Kurt chose a good time. He's a rogue, like the rest of them. And a coward. Didn't dare say he'd had enough of us and that it'd be more fun at the Doctor's ball. Probably knew we'd give him a rotten supper. That bastard hasn't changed.

KURT [*hastens in, right*] : My dear Edgar! Look, it's like this. The Doctor knows all about your heart —

CAPTAIN: Heart?

KURT: Yes. You've had a bad heart for some time. A hardening —

CAPTAIN: An ossifying of the heart?

KURT: And —

CAPTAIN: Is it dangerous?

KURT: Well —

CAPTAIN: It is dangerous!

KURT: Yes.

CAPTAIN: Death?

KURT: You must be very careful. First — no more cigars.

The CAPTAIN *throws away his cigar.*

KURT: And no more whisky. Then, you must go to bed.

CAPTAIN [*frightened*] : No, not that. Not bed. Then it's the end. Then one never gets up again. I'll sleep on the sofa tonight. What else did he say?

KURT: He was very friendly, and says he'll come at once if you ask him.

CAPTAIN: Friendly, was he, the hypocrite? I don't want to see him. Can I eat?

KURT: Not tonight. And for the next few days, only milk.

CAPTAIN: Milk? I can't stand the stuff.

KURT: You'll have to learn.

CAPTAIN: No, I'm too old to learn. [*Clutches his head.*] Ah! There it is again! [*Remains seated, staring.*]

ALICE [*to* KURT]: What did the Doctor say?

KURT: That he *may* die.

ALICE: Thank God!

KURT: Take care, Alice! Take care. And now, go and get a pillow and a blanket, and I'll lay him on the sofa. Then I'll sit in this chair, all night.

ALICE: And I?

KURT: You go to bed. Your presence seems to worsen his condition.

ALICE: Order, and I'll obey. I know you want to help us both. [*Goes towards exit, left.*]

KURT: Both, Alice. I'm taking no sides in this.

> *He picks up the water carafe and goes out right. The wind rises outside. Then the door upstage blows open and an* OLD WOMAN *of poor and disagreeable appearance peers in.*

CAPTAIN [*wakes, gets up and looks around*]: So! They've left me, the rogues. [*Sees the* OLD WOMAN *and is frightened.*] Who's that? What do you want?

OLD WOMAN: I only wanted to shut the door, kind sir.

CAPTAIN: Why? Why?

OLD WOMAN: Because it blew open just as I was going past.

CAPTAIN: You were going to steal, you old devil!

OLD WOMAN: There's not much to take here. Christine told me.

CAPTAIN: Christine!

OLD WOMAN: Good night, sir. Sleep well.

She shuts the door and goes. ALICE *enters left with pillows and a blanket.*

CAPTAIN: Who was that at the door? Was there someone?

ALICE: Yes, old Maia from the workhouse. She was just walking past.

CAPTAIN: Are you sure?

ALICE: Are you frightened?

CAPTAIN: I, frightened? Of course not.

ALICE: If you won't go to bed, you'd better lie here.

CAPTAIN [*goes and lies on the chaise-longue*]: I *want* to lie here. [*Tries to take* ALICE's *hand but she draws it away.*]

KURT *enters with the water carafe.*

CAPTAIN: Kurt, don't leave me.

KURT: I'll stay with you all night. Alice is going to bed.

CAPTAIN: Good night, then, Alice.

ALICE [*to* KURT]: Good night, Kurt.

KURT: Good night.

ALICE *goes.* KURT *takes a chair and sits by the* CAPTAIN.

KURT: Won't you take off your boots?

CAPTAIN: No! A warrior must always be ready for action.

KURT: Are you expecting a battle?

CAPTAIN: Perhaps. [*Sits up in his bed.*] Kurt! You are the only person I have opened my heart to. Listen. If I die tonight — remember my children.

KURT: I will.

CAPTAIN: Thank you. I trust you.

KURT: Can you explain why you trust me?

CAPTAIN: We haven't been friends, I don't believe in friendship, and our two families were born enemies and have always fought each other —

KURT: And yet you trust me!

CAPTAIN: Yes! And I don't know why. [*Silence.*] Do you think I am going to die?

KURT: Like everyone else. There'll be no exception made for you.

CAPTAIN: Are you bitter?

KURT: Yes. Are you afraid of death? The wheelbarrow and the garden?

CAPTAIN: Suppose it isn't the end!

KURT: Many think it's not.

CAPTAIN: What then?

KURT: Just surprises, I suppose.

CAPTAIN: But one knows nothing for sure.

KURT: No, that's just it. So one must be prepared for everything.

CAPTAIN: You aren't so stupid as to believe in hell?

KURT: Don't you, who are in the midst of it?

CAPTAIN: I was only speaking metaphorically.

KURT: The way you described yours wasn't metaphorical. Poetic or otherwise.

    Silence.

CAPTAIN: If you only knew the agonies I suffer.

KURT: Bodily?

CAPTAIN: No, they aren't bodily.

KURT: Then they must be spiritual. There's no third kind.
   Pause.

CAPTAIN [*raises himself in his bed.*]: I don't want to die!

KURT: Just now you were longing for annihilation.

CAPTAIN: Yes, if it's painless.

KURT: But it isn't.

CAPTAIN: Is this annihilation, then?

KURT: The beginning of it.

CAPTAIN: Good night.

KURT: Good night.

Scene 2

*The same. The lamp is beginning to gutter. Through
the windows and the glass panes of the upstage doors
can be seen an overcast morning. The sea is rolling.
A sentry stands at the battery as before. The
CAPTAIN is lying on the chaise-longue, asleep. KURT
sits on a chair beside him, pale and spent with lack of
sleep.*

ALICE: [*enters left*]: Is he asleep?

KURT: Yes, since sunrise.

ALICE: What sort of a night?

KURT: He's slept in snatches. But he's been talking so
much.

ALICE: What about?

KURT: He's been going on about religion like a schoolboy.
Seems to think he's solved the problems of existence.
Finally, towards dawn, he discovered the immortality of
the soul.

ALICE: *His* soul, of course.

KURT: Absolutely! He really is the most arrogant creature I've ever met. "*I* am, therefore God exists."

ALICE: So you've realized that. Look at those boots. With them he'd have trampled the earth flat, if he'd had the chance. With them he has trampled on other men's fields and flowers, other men's hearts and my brain. Now the wild boar feels the hunter's knife.

KURT: He'd be comic if he weren't tragic. It's strange, but in all his meannesses there's a kind of grandeur. Can't you find one good word to say about him?

ALICE [*sits*]: I could. But not for him to hear. One word to encourage him, and his arrogance exceeds all limits.

KURT: He can't hear anything. I've given him morphine.

ALICE: Well — he was born in a poor home, one of a large family. From an early age he had to support them by giving lessons, because his father was an idler — or worse. It must be hard for a young man to have to give up his youth to slave for a pack of ungrateful brats who weren't even his own. I remember first seeing him when I was a little girl — it was winter, twenty-five below zero, and he hadn't even an overcoat, though they all had. I thought it was noble, and I admired him for it, but his ugliness frightened me. He is unusually ugly, isn't he?

KURT: Yes — sometimes repulsively so. I noticed it particularly every time I quarrelled with him. And then, when he wasn't there, his image grew, took on strange forms and monstrous proportions. He literally began to haunt me.

ALICE: How do you suppose it must be for me, then? Oh, I suppose those first years as an officer must have been a martyrdom for him. He got help now and then, but he'll never admit it, and everything he could get he took as his due without a word of thanks.

KURT: We ought to speak charitably of him.

ALICE: After he's dead! Yes; well, then, I'll say no more.

KURT: Do you think he's evil?

ALICE: Yes. And yet, he can be kind and sensitive. But if he hates you, he's a monster.

KURT: Why didn't he become a major?

ALICE: Does it surprise you? They didn't want to have a man over them who'd already proved himself a tyrant under them! But you must never mention that. *He* says he didn't want to become a major. Did he say anything about the children?

KURT: Yes, he wanted to see Judith.

ALICE: I can imagine! Do you know who Judith is? She's the spit of him, and he's trained her to oppose me. Would you believe it, my own daughter has raised her hand against me.

KURT: Surely not?

ALICE: Hush! He's moving. I wonder if he heard us? He's cunning, too.

KURT: Yes — he's waking up.

ALICE: Doesn't he look like the devil himself! I'm frightened of him.

   Silence.

CAPTAIN [*stirs, wakes, stands up and looks around*]: It's morning. At last!

KURT: How are you feeling?

CAPTAIN: Bad.

KURT: Would you like a doctor?

CAPTAIN: No. I want to see Judith. My child.

KURT: Don't you think you should — make arrangements — before — in case — anything happens?

CAPTAIN: What do you mean? What should happen?

KURT: What can happen to everyone.

CAPTAIN: Oh, rubbish. I won't die that easily, believe me. Don't start celebrating in advance, Alice.

KURT: Think of your children. Make your will, so that at least your wife can be sure of her furniture.

CAPTAIN: You want her to inherit my possessions while I am still alive?

KURT: No. But if anything should happen, you don't want her to be thrown out on the road. Someone who for twenty-five years has cleaned, dusted and polished this furniture should have some right to it. Shall I get a lawyer?

CAPTAIN: No.

KURT: You're a cruel man. Crueller than I thought.

CAPTAIN [*falls helplessly on the bed*]: Ah! There it is again!

KURT: Go, Alice. There's little we can do here.

ALICE *goes.*

CAPTAIN [*comes to*]: Well, Kurt. How are you planning to arrange this quarantine?

KURT: Oh, I shall manage.

CAPTAIN: No, I'm in charge on this island, and you've got to deal with me. Don't forget that.

KURT: Have you ever seen a quarantine?

CAPTAIN: Have I? Yes, before you were born! And I'll give you some advice. Don't put the disinfection ovens too near the shore.

KURT: I thought they ought to be close to the water —

CAPTAIN: That shows how much you know about your job. Water is the natural element of germs. They thrive in it.

KURT: But salt water is necessary to cleanse away the impurities.

CAPTAIN: Imbecile! Well, as soon as you've found somewhere to live, you must bring your children to join you.

KURT: Do you think they'll come?

CAPTAIN: Of course, if you show yourself a man. It'll make a good impression on people here if you make it clear that you know your duties in that field —

KURT: I have always fulfilled my duties in that field.

CAPTAIN [*raises his voice*] : — In that field where your weakness is most painfully evident.

KURT: Haven't I told you — ?

CAPTAIN [*in full spate*] : I mean, one doesn't leave one's children like that —

KURT: Oh, carry on!

CAPTAIN: As your kinsman, and as the senior member of the family, I feel a certain duty to tell you the truth, even when it is painful. And you mustn't take offence —

KURT: Are you hungry?

CAPTAIN: Yes, I am!

KURT: Would you like something light?

CAPTAIN: No, something strong.

KURT: That'd finish you.

CAPTAIN: Isn't it enough to be ill, must one starve too?

KURT: That's the way it is.

CAPTAIN: And no drinking or smoking! Then life's not worth much.

KURT: Death demands sacrifices. Otherwise he comes at once.

ALICE [*enters with some bunches of flowers, telegrams and letters*] : These are for you. [*Throws the flowers on the desk.*]

CAPTAIN [*flattered*] : For me? May I see them?

ALICE: Yes, they're only from the junior officers, the band and the sentries.

CAPTAIN: You're jealous!

ALICE: Oh, no. If they were laurel wreaths, that would be different. But those you'll never get.

CAPTAIN: Hm! Here is a telegram from the Colonel. Read it, Kurt. At least he's a gentleman, though he is a little fool. This one's from — What's this? It's from Judith! Be so good as to telegraph her to come by the next ship. This one —! Well! One isn't without friends after all. It's a comfort that people think without fear or reproach of a sick man who deserves more recognition than he has been granted.

ALICE: I don't understand. Are they congratulating you on being ill?

CAPTAIN: Hyena!

ALICE [*to KURT*] : Yes, we had a doctor here who was so hated that when he left the island they gave a banquet— *after* he'd gone.

CAPTAIN: Put the flowers in vases. I am not a credulous man, and humanity is scum, but this simple homage, by God, it comes from the heart. It cannot but come from the heart.

ALICE: Imbecile!

KURT [*reads one of the telegrams*] : Judith says that she cannot come, because the steamer has been delayed by a storm.

CAPTAIN: Is that all?

KURT: Er — no. There is something more.

CAPTAIN: Out with it!

KURT: Well, she asks you not to drink so much.

CAPTAIN: My God! That's children for you. My only beloved daughter — my Judith! My idol!

ALICE: And your spit!

CAPTAIN: This is life. The best life has to offer. Shit!

ALICE: Well, you sowed this harvest yourself. You taught her to rebel against her mother, now she turns against her father. And you say there is no God!

CAPTAIN [*to* KURT]: What does the Colonel write?

KURT: He grants you leave from all duties forthwith.

CAPTAIN: Leave! I haven't asked for any leave.

ALICE: No, but I have.

CAPTAIN: I won't accept it!

ALICE: The arrangements have already been made.

CAPTAIN: I don't care!

ALICE: You see, Kurt. For this man no laws exist, no rules apply, no human authority matters. He stands above everything and everyone, the universe has been created for his private benefit, the sun and the moon are merely his messengers to carry his orders to the stars. That's my husband! This insignificant captain who couldn't even become a major, whose puffed-up pride is a laughing-stock to those who he supposes fear him — this coward who is afraid of the dark, and believes that all the discoveries of science are merely the build-up to his grand finale — a barrowload of manure, and that not of the top quality.

CAPTAIN [*fans himself with a bunch of flowers complacently, without listening to her*]: Have you invited Kurt to lunch?

ALICE: No.

CAPTAIN: Then go at once to the kitchen and grill the two best steaks you can find.

ALICE: Two?

CAPTAIN: I propose to have one too.

ALICE: But we are three.

CAPTAIN: You want one too? Very well, then; three.

ALICE: Where do you expect me to find them? Last night you invited Kurt to supper and there wasn't a crust of bread in the house. Kurt has had to sit up all night with you on an empty stomach and hasn't even had a cup of coffee, because we haven't got any and our credit is finished.

CAPTAIN: She's angry with me because I didn't die yesterday.

ALICE: No, because you didn't die twenty-five years ago. Because you didn't die before I was born.

CAPTAIN [to KURT]: Listen to her. That's what happens when you matchmake, my dear Kurt. Our marriage certainly wasn't arranged in heaven!

ALICE and KURT look at each other meaningfully.

CAPTAIN [gets up and walks towards the door]: However! Say what you may, I am going about my duty. [Puts on his old artillery helmet with bands. Fastens his sabre about his waist and puts on his greatcoat. ALICE and KURT try to stop him, but in vain.]

CAPTAIN: Get away from me! [Goes.]

ALICE: Yes, go! That's what you always do, turn your back when things become too much for you, and make your wife cover your retreat. Drunkard, braggart, liar! [Spits.]

KURT: Is there no limit to this?

ALICE [laughs]: You haven't seen the worst.

KURT: Worse than this?

ALICE: Don't ask me.

KURT: Where's he going now? And where does he find the strength?

ALICE: You may well ask. Oh, now he'll go down to his lieutenants to thank them for the flowers. And then he'll eat and drink with them. And he calls them scum! If you knew how many times he's been threatened with dismissal! It's only out of pity for his family that they've spared him. And he thinks it's because they're scared of him! And these wretched officers' wives who've tried to help us, he hates them and calls trash.

KURT: I must confess, I applied for this job in the hope of finding some peace down here by the sea. I had no idea how things were with you two —

ALICE: Poor Kurt. What will you do for food?

KURT: Oh, I'll get something at the Doctor's. But what about you? Can't I arrange something for you?

ALICE: He mustn't know, or he'll kill me.

KURT [*looks out through window*]: Look. He's standing on the ramparts. In this wind.

ALICE: One can't but pity him. That he is the way he is.

KURT: I pity both of you. But what is to be done?

ALICE: I don't know. A heap of bills has come too, which of course he didn't notice.

KURT: It can be a blessing not to be able to see, sometimes.

ALICE [*at the window*]: Now he's opened his coat and is letting the wind blow against his chest. He wants to die!

KURT: I don't think he does. Just now, when he felt his life was slipping away, he clutched on to mine, he began to smuggle his way into my private affairs, as though he wanted to worm into me and live my life.

ALICE: That's his way. He's a vampire, he likes to sink
his claws into other people's destinies, suck excitement
out of other lives, batten on others, because his own life
is so totally boring to him. Remember this, Kurt. Never
let him into your life, never let him know your friends,
or he'll take them from you and make them his. He's
a real demon at that. If he ever meets your children, you'll
soon find them regarding him as their father, they'll
follow his advice, he'll bring them up the way he wants,
and above all, he'll oppose every wish of yours.

KURT: Alice! Was it he who took my children from me,
when I parted from my wife?

ALICE: Since it's past — yes, it was he.

KURT: I suspected it, but I was never sure. So it was he!

ALICE: When you confided in him and sent him to mediate
with your wife, he started a flirtation with her and
taught her how she could get custody of the children.

KURT: Oh, God! God in heaven!

ALICE: You didn't know that side of him, did you?

Silence.

KURT: Do you know, last night — when he thought he was
going to die — he made me promise that I would remember
his children.

[ALICE: But surely you don't want to take revenge on my
children?

KURT: By keeping my promise? Very well, Alice. I shall
remember your children.]

ALICE: That would really be the most terrible revenge you
could take on him. There's nothing he loathes like mag-
nanimity.

KURT: Then I may find myself revenged by doing nothing.

ALICE: I love revenge as I love justice. It makes me happy
to see evil punished.

KURT: You still feel like that?

ALICE: I always shall. The day I forgive or love an enemy, call me a hypocrite.

KURT: Alice! It can be a duty sometimes to leave things unsaid, to turn a blind eye. It's what's called charity, and we all need that.

ALICE: I don't. I've no secrets to hide. I have always played clean.

KURT: That's a big claim.

ALICE: I could claim more. What have I not suffered for this man, whom I never loved — ?

KURT: Why did you marry him?

ALICE: Why did I? Because he took me. Seduced me. I don't know. And then, I wanted to get into society —

KURT: And gave up your work —

ALICE: Because society despised it. But you know, he cheated me. He promised me a good life, a beautiful home, and all I found was debts. The only gold I ever saw was on his uniform, and that wasn't real. He cheated me.

KURT: Alice! When a young man falls in love, he dreams of the future, and one must forgive him if his hopes don't always materialize. I have the same guilt on my conscience, but I don't regard myself as a cheat. What are you looking at out there?

ALICE: I'm looking to see if he has fallen.

KURT: Has he fallen?

ALICE: No such luck. Didn't I say, he always cheats me?

KURT: Well, I'll go and see the Doctor and the Governor.

ALICE [*sits by the window*]: You go, Kurt dear. I'll sit here and wait. I've learned to wait.

ACT TWO

Scene 1

*The same. Daylight. The sentry is on duty at the
battery as before.* ALICE *is seated in the armchair,
right. She is grey-haired.*

KURT [*knocks and enters, left*] : Good morning, Alice.

ALICE: Good morning, Kurt. Sit down.

KURT [*sits in the other armchair*] : The steamer's coming
in.

ALICE: I know what to expect, if he's on it.

KURT: He is. I saw the glint of his helmet. What has he
been doing in town?

ALICE: I can work it out. He put on his parade uniform,
which means he was going to see the Colonel, and he
took his suede gloves, so he must have been doing the
social round.

KURT: Did you notice how quiet he was yesterday? Since
he gave up drinking and over-eating he's been a different
person. Calm, reserved, considerate —

ALICE: I know. If that man had always been sober, he'd
have been a frightful danger to the world. Perhaps it's a
good thing he made himself ridiculous and harmless with
his whisky.

KURT: The genie in the bottle has tamed him! But have
you noticed how since death set its mark on him he has
acquired a kind of dignity, an exaltation? Perhaps the
prospect of mortality has caused him to rethink his views
on life.

ALICE: Don't you deceive yourself. He's plotting some

evil. And don't believe what he says. He's a premeditated liar, and a born intriguer —

KURT [*looks at her*] : Alice! What's this? You've become grey-haired in these two nights!

ALICE: No, Kurt. I've been that for a long time. It's just that I've given up dyeing it since my husband became a dead man. Twenty-five years in this fortress. Do you know it used to be a prison once?

KURT: A prison? Yes, you could guess that from the walls.

ALICE: And from my complexion. Even the children became prison-coloured in here.

KURT: It's difficult to imagine children playing within these walls.

ALICE: They didn't often play. And the two who died withered for lack of light.

KURT: What do you think will happen now?

ALICE: He'll attempt some *coup de grâce* against you and me. I saw a familiar glint in his eye when you read him that telegram from Judith. He'd have liked to take his revenge on her, but she's out of range so his hatred transferred to you.

KURT: What do you suppose he's planning?

ALICE: Hard to say. He has an incredible gift for — or luck at — nosing his way into other people's secrets. You must have noticed how all yesterday he lived himself into your quarantine, sucked vitality out of your children, devoured your children alive. I know him, Kurt. He's a cannibal. His own life is passing from him — or has passed —

KURT: I've got that impression too — that he's already on the other side. His face has a kind of phosphorescence, as though he was in a state of corruption. And his eyes flame like will-o'-the-wisps over graves or marshes. Here he is! Tell me — do you think he could possibly be jealous?

ALICE: No, he's too proud for that. "Show me the man I'd need to envy!" That's what he said.

KURT: Thank God for that. Even his vices have some merits! Shall I go out and greet him?

ALICE: No. Be offhand to him, or he'll think you're up to something. And when he starts lying, pretend to believe him. I know how to translate his lies, I can always find the truth [from them with my lexicon]. I feel something dreadful's going to happen . . . But Kurt, don't lose control of yourself. My only advantage in our long war has been that I've always been sober and had my wits about me. His whisky was his weakness! Now we'll see.

The CAPTAIN *enters left in parade uniform, helmet, cloak and white gloves, calm and grave, but pale and hollow-eyed. He stumbles forward and sits in his cloak and helmet far from* KURT *and* ALICE *on stage right. During the ensuing dialogue he holds his sabre between his knees.*

CAPTAIN: Good morning. Forgive my sitting down like this, but I am a little tired.

ALICE: Good morning.

KURT: Good to see you.

ALICE: How are you?

CAPTAIN: Fine. Just a little tired.

ALICE: What news from town?

CAPTAIN: Little but good. Amongst other people I saw the Doctor, and he says there's nothing wrong with me, that I can live for twenty years if I take care of myself.

ALICE [*to* KURT]: He's lying. [*To* CAPTAIN.] Well, that was good news, my dear.

CAPTAIN: Yes, it was.

Silence. The CAPTAIN *looks at* ALICE *and* KURT *as though asking them to speak.*

ALICE [*to* KURT]: Say nothing. Make him speak first and show his hand.

CAPTAIN [*to* ALICE]: Did you say something?

ALICE: No. I said nothing.

CAPTAIN [*slowly*]: Kurt, old chap —

ALICE [*to* KURT]: You see, he's off!

CAPTAIN: I — I was in town, as you know.

KURT *nods.*

CAPTAIN: I — er — made the acquaintance . . . amongst others . . . of a young cadet . . . [*hesitantly*] . . . in the artillery. [*Pause.* KURT *looks uneasy.*] Since . . . we're short of volunteers on this island, I arranged with the Colonel that he should be allowed to come here . . . This should please you particularly, when I inform you that it . . . was. . . your own son.

ALICE [*to* KURT]: The vampire! You see!

KURT: Under normal circumstances this news would please a father, but as things are I find it painful.

CAPTAIN: That I don't understand.

KURT: You don't need to. It's enough that I don't want it.

CAPTAIN: I see, that's how you feel! Well, you must know that the young man has been posted here and is now subject to my orders.

KURT: Then I shall make him apply for another regiment.

CAPTAIN: You can't; You have no rights concerning your son.

KURT: *I* have no — ?

CAPTAIN: No. The court has awarded them to his mother.

KURT: Then I shall contact his mother.

CAPTAIN: There is no need.

KURT: No need?

CAPTAIN: No. I have already done so. Yes!

KURT *starts to rise, but falls back in his chair.*

ALICE [*to* KURT]: Now he must die!

KURT: He *is* a cannibal.

CAPTAIN: So. That is that. [*Sharply, to* ALICE *and* KURT.] Did you say something?

ALICE: No. Have you become hard of hearing?

CAPTAIN: A little. But if you move closer, I'll tell you a secret. Between us two.

ALICE: There's no need for that. And a witness might be a good thing, for both parties.

CAPTAIN: Quite right! Witnesses are always a good thing. But first, is my will ready?

ALICE [*hands him a paper*]: The lawyer has drafted it.

CAPTAIN: In your favour? Good. [*Reads the will, then tears it carefully into pieces which he scatters on the floor.*] So. That's that. Yes!

ALICE [*to* KURT]: Have you ever seen a human being like him?

KURT: He isn't a human being.

CAPTAIN: Oh, Alice. I wanted to tell you something else —

ALICE [*uneasy*]: Yes?

CAPTAIN [*calmly, as before*]: In view of your oft-expressed wish to terminate the misery of your unhappy marriage, plus the complete lack of affection shown to your husband

and children, plus the negligence with which you have handled our domestic economy, I decided, during my visit to town, to deposit at the courthouse a petition for divorce.

ALICE: Oh? And your reason?

CAPTAIN [*still calmly*]: In addition to the reasons already listed, I have personal ones. Now that it has been established that I may live for another twenty years, I have decided to exchange my present unhappy state of matrimony for one better suited to my position. I intend to unite my destiny with that of a lady able to bring into my home not merely a wifely affection but also youth and — shall we say? — a hint of beauty.

ALICE [*takes off her ring and throws it at the* CAPTAIN]: Go ahead!

CAPTAIN [*picks up the ring and puts it in his waistcoat pocket*]: She throws away her ring. Will the witness be so good as to note this?

ALICE [*rises emotionally*]: And you intend to throw me out and put another woman in my house?

CAPTAIN: Yes.

ALICE: Right, then. Let's have it all out. Kurt — this man has been guilty of the attempted murder of his wife.

KURT: Attempted murder!

ALICE: Yes. He pushed me into the sea.

CAPTAIN: Without witnesses!

ALICE: He's lying. Judith saw it.

CAPTAIN: What's that got to do with it?

ALICE: She can testify.

CAPTAIN: No, she can't. She says she saw nothing.

ALICE: You've taught the child to lie!

CAPTAIN: I didn't need to. You'd taught her already.

ALICE: Have you been seeing Judith?

CAPTAIN: Yes.

ALICE: Oh, God! Oh, God!

CAPTAIN: The fortress has capitulated. The garrison is granted a safe conduct in ten minutes from now. [*Places his watch on the table.*] Ten minutes. By my watch. [*Clutches his heart and remains standing.*]

ALICE [*goes over and takes his arm*]: What is it?

CAPTAIN: I don't know.

ALICE: Do you want something? Would you like a drink?

CAPTAIN: Whisky? No, I don't want to die! Alice! [*Straightens himself.*] Don't touch me! Ten minutes, or the garrison will know what to expect. [*Draws his sabre.*] Ten minutes! [*Goes out upstage.*]

KURT: Who is this man?

ALICE: He's not a man, he's a demon.

KURT: What does he want with my son?

ALICE: He wants to have him as a hostage so that he can have you in his power. He wants to isolate you from the island's authorities. Do you know what this island is called by the people who live here? "The Little Hell."

KURT: I didn't know. Alice, you are the first woman who has ever made me feel sorry for her. All the others have seemed to me to deserve their fate.

ALICE: Don't abandon me now. Don't leave me, or he'll beat me. He has beaten me for twenty-five years — and in front of the children. He has even pushed me into the sea —

KURT: I can't try to be his friend any longer. I came here with no thought of malice. I was willing to forget how he'd humiliated me and blackened my name. I even for-

gave him when you told me it was he who'd taken my
children from me, because I could see he was sick and
dying. But now that he wants to take away my son, he
must die — he, or I.

ALICE: Good! Don't surrender the fortress, blow it to
hell and him with it, even if we have to go with him. I'll
find the gunpowder.

KURT: I wasn't angry with him when I came here. When I
felt your hatred infecting me, I thought of running away.
But now I feel an irresistible duty to hate this man as one
should hate evil. What can we do?

ALICE: I've learned my strategy from him. Get his enemies
together. Look for allies.

KURT: Fancy his managing to track down my wife! Why
didn't those two meet twenty-five years ago? That would
have been a match to make the earth tremble!

ALICE: But now they have met — and they must be parted.
I know his Achilles' heel — I've long suspected it —

KURT: Who is his worst enemy on this island?

ALICE: The Ordnance Officer.

KURT: Could we trust him?

ALICE: Yes. And he knows what I — yes, I know it too! — he
knows what the Sergeant-Major and my husband have been
up to together.

KURT: Up to? What do you mean?

ALICE: Embezzlement.

KURT: It's horrible. Look, I don't want to have anything
to do with this.

ALICE [laughs]: You can't strike an enemy?

KURT: I could once. Not any more.

ALICE: Why?

KURT: Because I have discovered that in the end, justice is always done.

ALICE: And you're prepared to wait? Till they've taken your son from you? Look at my grey hairs — yes, feel how thick they still are. He's planning to re-marry, so I am free to do the same. I am free! And in ten minutes he will be sitting down there, under arrest, down there! [*Stamps on the floor.*] Down there — and I shall dance above his head, I shall dance the *March of the Boyars*. [*Performs a few dance steps, with arms akimbo, and roars with laughter.*] And I'll play the piano, so that he shall hear! [*Hammers on the piano.*] Oh! the fortress will open its gates and the sentry with the drawn sword will no longer stand guard over me, but over him! Titti-tum-tum-ta, titti-tum-tum-tay! Him, him, him — !

KURT [*who has been watching her as though intoxicated*]: Alice! are you a devil like him?

ALICE [*jumps up on a chair and takes down the laurel wreaths*]: I shall wear these as I march out of this place. The laurels of triumph! And their ribbons will flutter — they're a little dusty, but they're evergreen. Like my youth. I'm not old, Kurt.

KURT [*his eyes aflame*]: You are a demon!

ALICE: In my little Hell! Look — I'll make myself ready. [*Loosens her hair.*] Give me two minutes to dress — two minutes to see the Ordnance Officer — and then, up goes the fortress!

KURT [*as before*]: You are a demon!

ALICE: You always used to say that when we were children. Do you remember, when we were children and said we'd marry each other! [*Laughs.*] You were shy, of course —

KURT [*earnestly*]: Alice!

ALICE: Yes, you were. And it suited you. You see — there

are coarse women who like shy men, and there — are said to
be shy men who like coarse women. You liked me a little
even then. Didn't you?

KURT: I don't know where I am. What are you?

ALICE: An actress who isn't scared by your conventions,
and is a woman! And now I am free, free, free! Turn your
back and I'll change my dress.

> *She begins to unbutton her dress.* KURT *rushes towards
> her, seizes her in his arms, lifts her high into the air
> and bites her on the throat. She screams. Then he
> throws her from him on to the sofa and runs out left.*

Scene 2

> *The same. Evening. The sentry can still be seen through
> the windows upstage. The laurel wreaths hang over the
> back of a chair. The ceiling lamp is lit. Soft music.*
>
> *The* CAPTAIN, *pale, hollow-eyed and, grizzled,
> in a worn uniform with riding boots, is seated at the
> desk playing patience.*
>
> *The interval music continues after the rise of the
> curtain until the other characters enter.*
>
> *The* CAPTAIN *continues with his game but now
> and then gives a start and looks up and listens anxiously.*
>
> *He seems unable to make his game come out;
> becomes impatient and sweeps the cards together. Then
> he goes to the window left, opens it and throws the
> cards out. The window remains open, shaking on its
> hinges.*
>
> *He goes to the cupboard, is frightened by the
> noise the window makes, turns round and looks to
> see what it is. Takes out three dark, square-sided
> whisky bottles, looks at them carefully, and throws
> them out of the window. Then he takes out some
> boxes of cigars, smells inside one of them, and throws
> them out through the window.*

*He takes off his glasses, dries them and tests them
to see how he sees with them. Then he throws them
out through the window, stumbles among the furniture
as though seeing badly, and lights a candelabra with
six candles that stands on the secretaire. Sees the
laurel wreaths, picks them up and goes towards the
window, but turns. Takes the piano cloth, and carefully
wipes the wreaths, takes some pins from the desk
and re-fixes the corners, then puts them all on a chair.
Goes to the piano, strikes the keys with his fists, shuts
the keyboard and throws the key through the window.
Then he lights the candles on the piano. Goes to the
whatnot, takes his wife's photograph, looks at it, tears
it up and throws the pieces on to the floor. The window
shakes on its hinges and frightens him again. He calms
himself, takes the photographs of his son and daughter,
kisses them lightly and stuffs them in his breast
pocket. The other photographs he sweeps to the floor
with his elbow and kicks into a heap with his boot.*

*Then he sits, tired, at the desk and feels his heart.
He lights the writing candles and sighs. Stares as
though seeing unpleasing visions. Gets up and goes to
the secretaire, opens the flap, takes out a bundle of
letters fastened with blue silk ribbons and throws
them into the stove. Shuts the secretaire. The telegraph taps a single stroke, then falls silent. The
CAPTAIN starts fearfully and stands with his hand on
his heart, listening. But hearing nothing more from
the telegraph, he listens towards the door left. Goes
over and opens it, takes a step inside and comes out
with a cat on his arm which he strokes along its back.
Then he goes out right. The music ceases.*

*ALICE enters upstage, dressed for walking with
her hair black, a hat and gloves. She looks around,
surprised at the many candles. KURT enters left,
nervous.*

ALICE: It looks like Christmas here.

KURT: Well?

ALICE [*holds out her hand for him to kiss*] : Thank me. [*He kisses her hand, unwillingly.*] Six witnesses, four of them irrefutable. The application has been despatched and the reply will come on the telegraph — here, into the heart of the fortress.

KURT: I see.

ALICE: Say "Thank you", not "I see".

KURT: Why has he lit so many candles?

ALICE: Because he's afraid of the dark, of course. Look at the telegraph! Doesn't it look like the handle of a coffee-mill? I grind, I grind, and the beans crunch. Like extracting a tooth —

KURT: What's he been doing in this room?

ALICE: It looks as though he's been making preparations to go. Down into the cells, that's where you'll go!

KURT: Alice, don't talk like that. I think it's horrible. He used to be my friend when we were young, and he was often kind to me when I was in trouble. I feel sorry for him.

ALICE: What about me? I did nothing to anyone and had to sacrifice my career for this monster.

KURT: That career of yours. Was it so brilliant?

ALICE [*furious*] : What the hell do you mean? Do you know who I am, or who I was?

KURT: Now, now. Don't get angry.

ALICE: Are you beginning too, already?

KURT: Already?

> ALICE *throws her arms round his neck and kisses him. He takes her in his arms and bites her on the neck so that she screams.*

ALICE: You're biting me!

KURT [*beside himself*]: Yes, I want to bite your neck and suck your blood like a stoat! You have woken the beast in me. I tried for years to stifle it by denying and tormenting myself. When I came here I thought myself a little better than you two — but now I am the meanest of us all. Since I saw you as you really are, in all your nakedness, since lust distorted my sight, I realize the full power of evil — it makes the ugly seem beautiful, the good seem ugly and weak. I want to strangle you — with a kiss! [*Embraces her.*]

ALICE [*shows her left hand*]: Do you see the mark of the bond from which you liberated me? I was a slave. Now I am free.

KURT: But I shall bind you —

ALICE: You?

KURT: I.

[ALICE: I thought for a moment you were —

KURT: Getting religious?

ALICE: Yes. The other day you began to talk about the Fall —

KURT: Did I?]

ALICE: And I thought you had come to preach at me —

KURT: You thought that? In an hour we shall be in town. Then you shall see what kind of a man I am —

ALICE: Tonight let us go to the theatre. Let us show ourselves. Don't you see? If I run away, the shame will be his.

KURT: I begin to understand. It isn't enough to put him in prison —

ALICE: No, it isn't enough. I want him shamed too.

KURT: A strange world. You commit the deed of shame, but he must bear it.

ALICE: That's the world's fault.

KURT: These walls! It's as though they'd soaked in all the evil of everyone who's ever been imprisoned here! One needs only to breathe here to be infected. While you are thinking of the theatre and supper, I have been thinking of my son.

ALICE [*strikes him on the mouth with her glove*]: Fool!

KURT *raises his hand to strike her back.*

ALICE [*shrinks*]: Charming!

KURT: Forgive me.

ALICE: On your knees, then. [*He kneels.*] On your face! [*He presses his forehead to the floor.*] Kiss my foot! [*He kisses her foot.*] And never do that again. Get up!

KURT [*gets up*]: What have I come to? Where am I?

ALICE: You know quite well.

KURT [*looks around in horror*]: I think I'm —

CAPTAIN [*enters right, dejected, supporting himself on a stick*]: May I speak with Kurt? Alone.

ALICE: Is it about the safe-conduct?

CAPTAIN [*sits at the sewing-table*]: Kurt, will you please sit with me for a little? Alice, will you grant us a moment's — peace?

ALICE: What's this? Here's a change. [*To* KURT.] By all means, sit down. [KURT *sits unwillingly.*] And hearken to the voice of age and wisdom. If a telegram comes, leave it to me. [*Goes out left.*]

CAPTAIN [*after a pause, gravely*]: Can you understand the purpose of a life like mine? Like ours?

KURT: No. As little as I understand my own.

CAPTAIN: Then what is the meaning of this chaos?

KURT: In my better moments I have believed that the

meaning of life is just that. That we should not know
the meaning, and yet should bow to it —

CAPTAIN: If I have no fixed point outside myself, how
can I bow to it?

KURT: Correct. But you, as a mathematician, should
surely be able to find that unknown point, given certain
data —

CAPTAIN: I have looked for it — and have not found it.

KURT: Then your calculations have been at fault. You
must start again.

CAPTAIN: I will. Tell me, where did you find such resignation?

KURT: I have none left. Don't overrate me.

CAPTAIN: As you may possibly have noticed, I have
understood the art of living to be a question of blotting
out the past. Forget, and go on living. When I was young
I made a little bag and stuffed into it all my humiliations,
and when it was full I threw it into the sea. I don't
believe any mortal being has suffered as many humiliations
as I have. But when I blotted them out and went on living,
they ceased to exist.

KURT: I've noticed what kind of a life you've created for
yourself. And for those around you.

CAPTAIN: How else could I have lived? How could I have
stood it? [Clutches at his heart.]

KURT: How are you feeling?

CAPTAIN: Bad. [Pause.] Then there comes a moment
when the ability to create, as you call it, stops. And then
reality stands forth in all its nakedness. It's terrifying.
[Now he speaks with an old man's tearfulness in his voice,
and drooping lower jaw.] You see, my dear friend . . .
[Controls himself and speaks with his normal voice.] Forgive me. When I was in town just now and spoke with the

Doctor — [*Tearfully again.*] He said I was all to pieces — [*In normal voice.*] And that I couldn't live long.

KURT: Did he say *that*?

CAPTAIN: Yes, he said that.

KURT: Then it wasn't true?

CAPTAIN: What? Oh, yes, that . . . No, it wasn't true.

   Pause.

KURT: Was the other thing a lie too?

CAPTAIN: How do you mean, old chap?

KURT: That my son was to be ordered here?

CAPTAIN: I've never heard any mention of that.

KURT: You know, your ability to forget the past is quite unbelievable!

CAPTAIN: Old chap, I don't understand what you mean.

KURT: Then you *are* all to pieces.

CAPTAIN: Yes, there isn't much left.

KURT: Perhaps you haven't petitioned to divorce your wife, either?

CAPTAIN: Divorce? No, never mentioned it.

KURT [*gets up*]: Then you admit you've been lying?

CAPTAIN: Old chap, you use such strong words. We all need a little indulgence.

KURT: You've realized that?

CAPTAIN [*firmly, in a clear voice*]: Yes, I have realized that. Forgive me, Kurt. Forgive me everything.

KURT: Bravely spoken. But I have nothing to forgive you. And I'm not the man you think, any longer. Least of all worthy to accept your confessions.

CAPTAIN [*in a clear voice*]: Life was so strange! So hostile,

so cruel — ever since childhood. People were so cruel, so
that I became cruel too — [KURT *walks over uneasily and
glances at the telegraph.*] What are you looking at?

KURT: Can one shut off a telegraph machine?

CAPTAIN: Not easily.

KURT [*with rising unease*]: Who is Sergeant-Major Östberg?

CAPTAIN: He's an honest chap. Bit of a dealer, of course.

KURT: Who is the Ordnance Officer, then?

CAPTAIN: Oh, he's my enemy, all right. Not a bad fellow
really, though.

KURT [*looks out through the window, where a lantern can
be seen moving*]: What are they doing with that lantern
out there by the guns?

CAPTAIN: Is there a lantern?

KURT: Yes, and people moving.

CAPTAIN: Probably what we call a welcoming committee.

KURT: What's that?

CAPTAIN: A platoon with a corporal. Some poor devil's
going to be arrested.

KURT: Oh.

   Pause.

CAPTAIN: Well, now that you know Alice, what do you
think of her?

KURT: I can't say. I just don't understand people at all. I
find her as inexplicable as I find you — and myself! I'm
getting to the age when if one's wise one admits one knows
nothing, and understands nothing. But when I see something happen, I want to know the reason. Why did you
push her into the sea?

CAPTAIN: I don't know. It just seemed to me quite

natural when she stood there on the jetty that she should go in.

KURT: Have you never regretted it?

CAPTAIN: Never.

KURT: That's strange.

CAPTAIN: Yes, it is. So strange that I can't believe it was I who could have done such a paltry thing.

KURT: Did it never occur to you that she'd get her revenge?

CAPTAIN: God knows she has. And I find that equally natural.

KURT: How have you come to be so cynically resigned in such a short space of time?

CAPTAIN: Since I looked death in the eyes, I have seen life from a different standpoint. Kurt, if you had to judge between Alice and me, which would you say was right?

KURT: Neither. I feel infinite pity for you both. Perhaps a little more for you.

CAPTAIN: Give me your hand, Kurt.

KURT [*holds out one hand and puts the other on the* CAPTAIN's *shoulder*]: Old friend!

ALICE [*enters left, carrying a parasol*]: Charming! Did I hear the word friend? Hasn't the telegram come?

KURT [*coldly*]: No.

ALICE: This delay's making me impatient, and when I get impatient I hurry things up. Look, Kurt. I'm going to finish him off now, and this'll settle him. First, I load — I know the drill, if anyone does, the famous rifle-drill that *didn't* sell five thousand copies. Then I take aim, fire! [*She aims the parasol.*] How is your new wife? That young, beautiful, unknown girl? You don't know. But I know how my lover is. [*Puts her arms around* KURT's *neck and kisses him. He pushes her away.*] He's splendid, but he's still shy. [*To the* CAPTAIN.] You scum, whom I never loved, you were too vain to be jealous, you never saw how I led you by the snout!

The CAPTAIN *draws his sabre and stumbles at her, hewing, but strikes only the furniture.*

ALICE: Help! Help!

KURT *stands motionless.*

CAPTAIN [*falls, the sabre in his hand*]: Judith! Avenge me!

ALICE: He's dying. Thank God!

KURT *moves towards the upstage door.*

CAPTAIN [*gets up*]: Not yet! [*Sheathes his sabre, goes over and sits in the chair by the sewing-table.*] Judith! Judith!

ALICE [*goes towards* KURT]: Now I'm going. With you.

KURT [*pushes her away so that she falls on her knees*]: Go to hell, whence you came! Goodbye. For ever.

CAPTAIN: Don't leave me, Kurt! She'll kill me.

ALICE: Kurt! Don't leave me! Don't leave us!

KURT: Goodbye. [*Goes.*]

ALICE [*changes her tone*]: What a wretch! There's a friend for you!

CAPTAIN [*gently*]: Forgive me, Alice, and come here. Come quickly!

ALICE: That man is the most contemptible and hypocritical wretch I have ever met in my life. At least you're a man.

CAPTAIN: Alice, listen to me. I can't live for long.

ALICE: Oh?

CAPTAIN: The Doctor told me.

ALICE: Then the other thing was untrue too?

CAPTAIN: Yes.

ALICE [*desperate*]: Oh, God! What have I done?

CAPTAIN: Nothing is irreparable.

ALICE: Yes. This is irreparable.

CAPTAIN: Nothing is irreparable, as long as one blots out the past and goes on living.

ALICE: But the telegram! The telegram!

CAPTAIN: What telegram?

ALICE [*on her knees beside him*]: Are we damned? Did this have to happen? I've destroyed myself — I've destroyed both of us! Why did you let yourself be fooled? And why did this man have to come and tempt me? We are lost. Everything could have been all right — you could have forgiven me —

CAPTAIN: What is it that cannot be forgiven? What have I not forgiven you?

ALICE: I know. But this time, there's no help.

CAPTAIN: I know how inventive you are in evil, but I can't guess what you —

ALICE: Oh, if I could undo it! If I could undo it, I would take care of you! Edgar, I would love you!

CAPTAIN: Listen to her! What's going on?

ALICE: Do you think no one can help us? Yes — no mortal can —

CAPTAIN: Who could, then?

ALICE [*looks the* CAPTAIN *in the eyes*]: I don't know. Think — what will become of the children? Their name will be dishonoured —

CAPTAIN: Have you dishonoured our name?

ALICE: No, not I! Not I! But — they'll have to leave school.

And when they go out into the world, they'll be alone like us, and evil like us. . . Then you didn't meet Judith either, I realize now?

CAPTAIN: No. But blot that out too.

The telegraph taps. ALICE jumps up.

ALICE [*screams*]: Now it's happening! Don't listen to it!

CAPTAIN [*calmly*]: I won't listen to it, dearest child. Calm yourself —

ALICE [*stands by the telegraph and stands on tiptoe to look out through the window*]: Don't listen! Don't listen!

CAPTAIN [*holds his ears*]: I'm holding my ears, Lisa, my child.

ALICE [*on her knees with outstretched hands*]: God help us! They're coming to arrest you. [*Weeps.*] God in heaven!

She moves her lips as though in silent prayer. The telegraph is still tapping gently, and a long ribbon of paper has crept from it. Then it falls quiet again.

ALICE [*gets up, tears off the strip of paper and reads it silently. Then she glances upwards, goes over and kisses the* CAPTAIN *on the forehead*]: It's all right. It was nothing. [*Sits in the other chair and sobs violently into her handkerchief.*]

CAPTAIN: What secrets have you got there?

ALICE: Don't ask. It's over now.

CAPTAIN: As you wish, my child.

ALICE: You wouldn't have spoken like that three days ago. Why now?

CAPTAIN: Alice. That first time I fell, I was a short while on the other side of the grave. What I saw I have forgotten, but the impression remained.

ALICE: What was it?

CAPTAIN: Hope of a better —

ALICE: A better —?

CAPTAIN: Yes. I have never really believed that this was life. This is death. Or something even worse —

ALICE: And we — ?

CAPTAIN: It was our destiny to torment each other — it seems.

ALICE: Have we tormented each other enough?

CAPTAIN: Yes, I think so. I think so. [*Looks around.*] Shall we tidy up after us? And leave things clean?

ALICE [*gets up*]: If we can.

CAPTAIN [*looks around the room*]: It won't be done in a day. Not in a day.

ALICE: But some time —

CAPTAIN: Let us hope so.

Pause.

CAPTAIN [*sits again*]: So you didn't escape this time. But you didn't get me put away either. [*She is amazed.*] Yes, I knew you wanted to have me put in prison. But I blot that out. You've done worse things than that. [*She is silent.*] You know, I didn't embezzle that money.

ALICE: And now you propose that I shall be your sick-nurse?

CAPTAIN: If you wish to be.

ALICE: What other choice have I?

CAPTAIN: I don't know.

ALICE [*sits limply, in despair*]: But this is eternal hell. Is there no end, then?

CAPTAIN: Yes, if we are patient. Perhaps when death comes, life begins.

ALICE: If only that could be true!

Pause.

CAPTAIN: You think Kurt was a hypocrite?

ALICE: I'm sure of it.

CAPTAIN: I don't think so. But everyone who comes near us becomes evil, and moves on. Kurt was weak, and evil is strong. [*Pause.*] How banal life is nowadays! In the old days one fought, now one merely threatens. I'm pretty sure that in three months we will celebrate our silver wedding — with Kurt to propose the toast — and the Doctor and Gerda will be there . . . The Ordnance Officer will make a speech, and the Sergeant-Major will lead the cheers. And if I know the Colonel, he'll invite himself. Yes, you laugh. But do you remember Adolf's wedding — that fellow in the Hussars? The bride had to wear her ring on her right hand because the bridegroom, in a fit of tender passion, had chopped off the third finger of her left hand with a jewelled penknife.

> ALICE *holds her handkerchief to her mouth to stifle a laugh.*

CAPTAIN: Are you crying? No, I believe you're laughing! Yes, child, sometimes we cry and sometimes we laugh. Which is the more fitting? Don't ask me, The other day I read in a newspaper that a man had been divorced seven times, *ergo* had married seven times — and in the end ran away at the age of ninety-eight and re-married his first wife. There's love for you! Is life serious or just a hoax? I don't know. When it's a farce it can be a nightmare, when it's serious it can be quite soothing and tolerable. But when you finally decide to play it serious, someone always comes along and treats you like a clown. Kurt for instance. Do you want to celebrate our silver wedding? [ALICE *is silent.*] Say yes, Alice. They'll laugh at us, but what of that? We'll laugh too — or be serious. Whichever way it turns out.

ALICE: Yes. Let us.

CAPTAIN [*earnestly*]: Well, then. Our silver jubilee. [*Gets up.*] Blot out the past and go on living. Well. Let's go on.

PART II

(1900)

CHARACTERS

EDGAR, the CAPTAIN

ALICE

KURT

ALLAN, KURT's son

JUDITH, EDGAR's daughter

THE LIEUTENANT

This translation was first performed in London on 15 June 1978 by the Royal Shakespeare Company at the Aldwych Theatre.
The cast was:

EDGAR	Emrys James
ALICE	Sheila Allen
KURT	Alan David
ALLAN	Richard Dennington
JUDITH	Lynsey Baxter
LIEUTENANT	Michael Bertenshaw

Designed by Mary Moore
Directed by John Caird

Scene 1

*An oval drawing-room in white and gold. The rear
wall is broken by glass doors, which stand open to
reveal the garden terrace outside, with a balustrade of
stone pillars and blue-white earthenware pots
containing petunias and geraniums. This terrace is part
of the garden walk. Beyond can be seen the shore
battery with a sentry. In the distance, the open sea.*

*In the room, to the left, stands a gilt sofa, with a
table and chairs. To the right, a grand piano, a desk
and a fireplace. Downstage, an American armchair. By
the desk, a copper standard-lamp, with a table attached.
Various old oil-paintings on the walls.*

*ALLAN is seated at the desk, engaged in mathe-
matical calculations. JUDITH enters through the
upstage door in a short summer dress, with a pigtail
down her back, her hat in one hand and a tennis racket
in the other. ALLAN gets up, grave and respectful.*

JUDITH [*earnest yet friendly*]: Why won't you come and
play tennis?

ALLAN [*shy, fighting his feelings*]: I'm so busy —

JUDITH: Didn't you see I put my bicycle *facing* the oak,
not away from it?

ALLAN: Yes, I saw that.

JUDITH: Well, what does that mean?

ALLAN: It means — that you want me to come and play
tennis — but my duties — I have these problems to solve,
and your father is a pretty severe taskmaster.

JUDITH: Do you like him?

ALLAN: Yes, I do. He takes an interest in all his pupils —

JUDITH: He takes an interest in everyone and everything. Do you want to come?

ALLAN: You know I want to. But I shouldn't.

JUDITH: I'll ask Daddy to give you permission.

ALLAN: Don't do that. People'll only talk.

JUDITH: You think I can't manage him? He wants what I want.

ALLAN: That's because you're so hard. Yes!

JUDITH: You should be, too.

ALLAN: My family aren't wolves.

JUDITH: Then you'll become a sheep.

ALLAN: I'd rather that.

JUDITH: Tell me, why won't you come and play tennis?

ALLAN: You know.

JUDITH: Tell me, though. The Lieutenant?

ALLAN: Yes. You don't care a bit about me, but you don't enjoy being with the Lieutenant unless I'm around so you can see me suffer.

JUDITH: Am I so cruel? I didn't know.

ALLAN: Now you do know.

JUDITH: Then I'll be good from now on. I don't want to be cruel, I don't want to seem bad — to you.

ALLAN: You only say that to get me back in your power. I'm already your slave, but you aren't content with that, your slave has to be tortured and thrown to the beasts! You've already got *him* in your claws, what do you want with me, then? Let me go my way, and you go yours.

JUDITH: Are you telling me to get out? [ALLAN *does not reply*.] All right, I'll go. We'll have to meet occasionally because we're cousins, but I won't bother you.

ALLAN *sits at the desk and returns to his calculations.*
JUDITH, *instead of going, comes into the room and*
gradually approaches the desk where ALLAN *is*
sitting.

JUDITH: Don't be frightened, I'll go in a minute. I just
wanted to see what kind of a house the Quarantine
Master has. [*Looks around.*] White and gold! A piano,
Bechstein! Mm! We're still in the fortress, now Daddy's
pensioned. The fortress, where Mother has sat for
twenty-five years. And we're there on charity. You're
rich, all you lot —

ALLAN [*quietly*]: We're not rich.

JUDITH: You say that, but you're always so smartly
dressed — and whatever you wear suits you. Are you
listening to me? [*Goes closer.*]

ALLAN [*submissively*]: I'm listening.

JUDITH: How can you listen when you sit doing sums, or
whatever you are doing?

ALLAN: I don't listen with my eyes.

JUDITH: Your eyes, yes. Have you looked at them in a
mirror?

ALLAN: Go away.

JUDITH: You despise me!

ALLAN: My dear girl, I don't think about you.

JUDITH [*comes closer*]; Archimedes, sitting at his sums as
the soldiers break in and cut him down! [*Ruffles his papers
with her racket.*]

ALLAN: Don't touch my papers!

JUDITH: That's what Archimedes said. Now you're getting
ideas, of course. You think I can't live without you.

ALLAN: Why can't you leave me in peace?

JUDITH: Be nice, and I'll help you with your exam —

ALLAN: You?

JUDITH: Yes. I know the examiners —

ALLAN [*sternly*]: What do you mean?

JUDITH: Don't you know that it helps to have the examiners on your side?

ALLAN: Meaning your father and the Lieutenant?

JUDITH: And the Colonel.

ALLAN: You mean that with your help I needn't do any work?

JUDITH: That's a nasty translation.

ALLAN: Of a nasty original.

JUDITH: You're beastly!

ALLAN: I'm doing this for your sake, and mine. I'm ashamed I even listened to you. Why don't you go?

JUDITH: Because I know you like my company. Yes, you always manage to walk past my window! You've always some errand that takes you to town on the same steamer as me, you can't go out in a boat without me to work the sail.

ALLAN [*shyly*]: A young girl shouldn't talk like that.

JUDITH: Do you think I'm a child?

ALLAN: Sometimes you're a delightful child, sometimes a scheming woman. You seem to have chosen me to be your sheep.

JUDITH: You are a sheep, so I shall protect you.

ALLAN [*gets up*]: A wolf is always a bad sheepdog. You want to eat me — that's the real truth. You're willing to stake your beautiful eyes in return for my head.

JUDITH: Oh, you have noticed my eyes? I didn't think you were that bold.

ALLAN *gathers his papers and makes to go out right.*
JUDITH *puts herself between him and the door.*

ALLAN: Get out of my way, or —

JUDITH: Or?

ALLAN: If you were a boy, I'd — ! But you're a girl.

JUDITH: Well?

ALLAN: If you had an atom of pride, you'd have gone. I
as good as kicked you out.

JUDITH [*walks angrily towards the glass doors*]: I'll make
you sorry for this!

ALLAN: I don't doubt it.

JUDITH: I'll — make — you — sorry — for — this. [*Goes.*]

KURT [*enters left*]: Where are you going, Allan?

ALLAN: Is it you?

KURT: Who was that who ran out in such a hurry?

ALLAN: Judith.

KURT: She's a bit explosive. But she's a good girl.

ALLAN: When a girl is hard and ruthless, people always
say she's a good girl.

KURT: You mustn't be such a Puritan, Allan. Aren't you
happy with your new relations?

ALLAN: I like Uncle Edgar —

KURT: Yes, he has many good sides. And your other
teachers? The Lieutenant, for example?

ALLAN: He's so moody. Sometimes he seems to have
some grudge against me.

KURT: Oh, no. You imagine too much. Don't brood so.
Do your work, be polite to people and let them be themselves.

ALLAN: Well, I do, but — they won't leave me in peace.
They suck one in — just like those octopuses down by the
jetty. They don't bite, but they stir up a whirlpool that
pulls one down —

KURT [*gently*] : I think you tend to look on the dark side
of things. Aren't you happy here with me? Is there something you miss?

ALLAN: I've never known such kindness, but — there's
something here that suffocates me.

KURT: Here by the sea? Don't you like the sea?

ALLAN: The open sea, yes. But the water here's different,
it's full of snare-grass, octopuses, jellyfish, nettlefish or
whatever they call them.

KURT: You shouldn't sit indoors so much. Go out and
play tennis.

ALLAN: I don't want to.

KURT: You're angry with Judith, I can see.

ALLAN: Judith?

KURT: You're so touchy about people. One mustn't be
that, or one finds oneself alone.

ALLAN: I'm not touchy, but — I feel as though I was a
log at the bottom of the wood-pile, having to wait my
turn to get into the fire. Everything's on top of me, and
it presses, and presses —

KURT: Wait till your turn comes. The pile will grow
smaller —

ALLAN: Yes, but so slowly, so slowly! Ugh! And meanwhile I lie here mouldering.

KURT: It's no fun being young. And yet one envies you —

ALLAN: Does one? Would you like to change places with
me?

KURT: No, thank you!

ALLAN: Do you know what the worst thing is? Having to sit and keep quiet while old people talk nonsense! Sometimes I *know* I know more about something than them, but I have to keep my mouth shut. Sorry, I don't think of you as old.

KURT: Why not?

ALLAN: Perhaps because I've really only just got to know you —

KURT: And because — you had a different picture of me before?

ALLAN: Yes.

KURT: I imagine that during those years we were parted you didn't always have the warmest feelings about me?

ALLAN: No.

KURT: Did you ever see a photograph of me?

ALLAN: Only one. And that was very unflattering.

KURT: And old?

ALLAN: Yes.

KURT: Ten years ago I went grey-haired in a single night. Later it returned to its old colour. Of its own accord. Let's talk about something else. Look. Here comes your aunt. My cousin. What do you think of her?

ALLAN: I'd rather not say.

KURT: Then I won't ask.

ALICE [*enters in a very light-coloured summer walking-dress, with a parasol*] : Good morning, Kurt. [*She gives a look signifying that* ALLAN *should leave them.*]

KURT [*to* ALLAN] : Leave us.

> ALLAN *goes out right.* ALICE *sits on a sofa left,* KURT *in a chair beside her.*

ALICE [*irritably*] : He'll be here in a moment, so you needn't feel embarrassed.

KURT: Why should I be?

ALICE: You're such a moralist.

KURT: Only as regards myself.

ALICE: Oh, yes! Once I forgot myself, when I thought I saw you as a liberator, but you kept your head, so we can forget what never happened.

KURT: Forget it, then.

ALICE: Yes, but I don't think *he* has forgotten —

KURT: You mean, that night he had a heart attack? And you thought he was dead and started celebrating prematurely?

ALICE: Yes. And he recovered. But when he gave up drinking he learned to keep silent, and now he's terrifying. He's up to something I don't understand —

KURT: Alice. Your husband is a decent ass, who shows me nothing but kindness —

ALICE: Beware of his kindnesses. I know them.

KURT: Alice, please —

ALICE: So he's fooled you too. Don't you see the danger, can't you sense the traps?

KURT: No.

ALICE: Then you haven't a hope.

KURT: Oh, really!

ALICE: It's extraordinary. I sit here and see disaster creeping up on you like a cat. I point it out to you, but you won't see it.

KURT: Allan can't see it either, and he has no reason to be biased. Though I admit he can only see Judith. But that should be a guarantee of a good relationship.

ALICE: Do you know Judith?

KURT: A little flirt with plaits down her back and skirts
that are too short —

ALICE: Exactly! But I saw her dressed up the other day in
a long skirt and what I saw then was a young lady — not so
young, either, when her hair was up.

KURT: She is a little forward for her age, I admit.

ALICE: And she's playing with Allan.

KURT: That's all right, as long as it's just play.

ALICE: Oh, that's all right, is it? [*Pause.*] Edgar will be
here in a moment. He'll sit in that armchair. He's got an
obsession about that. You be careful he doesn't steal it.

KURT: He's welcome to it.

ALICE: Let him sit there, then we can stay here. And when
he starts talking — he's always garrulous in the morning —
when he says things that seem meaningless, I'll translate
them for you.

KURT: Oh, Alice, you *worry* too much, you worry *too
much*. What have I got to fear as long as I do this quarantine job properly and don't offend anyone?

ALICE: You believe in justice and honour and all that?

KURT: Yes, experience has taught me to. Once I used to
believe the opposite. It cost me dearly.

ALICE: Here he is.

KURT: I've never seen you scared before.

ALICE: My courage was only ignorance. Of the danger.

KURT: The danger? You'll start scaring me soon.

ALICE: If only I could. Here he is.

The CAPTAIN *enters upstage in mufti — a black,
buttoned morning coat, a military cap, a stick with*

*a silver handle. He greets them with a nod and sits
in the armchair.*

ALICE [*to* KURT]: Let him speak first.

CAPTAIN: This is a superb chair you have, my dear Kurt.
Quite superb.

KURT: You can have it if you like. As a gift.

CAPTAIN: I didn't mean that —

KURT: But I do. Think of all you've given me.

CAPTAIN [*garrulously*]: Oh, rubbish . . . And when I sit
here, I look out over the whole island, over the promenades,
I see all the people on their verandahs, all the ships that
sail on the sea, coming in and going out. You've certainly
managed to get the best corner of this island, and it isn't
exactly a Garden of Eden. No, it's known as Little Hell,
and Kurt has built himself a Paradise here — without his
Eve, of course, whose coming put an end to Paradise. By
the way, do you know this was once a royal hunting-
lodge?

KURT: So I have heard.

CAPTAIN: You live like a king yourself. But I do wish
people wouldn't say you have me to thank for it.

ALICE [*to* KURT]: You see. Now he's trying to steal you.

KURT: I have much to thank you for.

CAPTAIN: Oh, rubbish. By the way, did you get those
cases of wine?

KURT: Yes.

CAPTAIN: And you like them?

KURT: Very much. Please thank your shipper and tell him
so.

CAPTAIN: He always sells first-class stuff —

ALICE [*to* KURT]: At second-class prices, and you have
to pay the difference.

CAPTAIN: What did you say, Alice?

ALICE: I? Nothing.

CAPTAIN: Well. When this post of Quarantine Master was established, I considered applying for it myself. So I began to study the subject.

ALICE [to KURT]: He's lying.

CAPTAIN [boastfully]: The views held by the authorities regarding the problems of disinfection struck me as obsolete. I preferred those of the Neptunists, so called because they favour the water method —

KURT: Forgive me, but I remember clearly that it was I who advocated the water method, and you who believed in the ovens.

CAPTAIN: I? Nonsense.

ALICE [loudly]: Yes, I remember that too.

CAPTAIN: You?

KURT: I remember it clearly, because —

CAPTAIN [interrupts]: Well, it's just possible, but in any case it's irrelevant. We have now reached the point where a new situation — [To KURT who is about to interrupt.] If you don't mind! — has arisen — and the science of quarantine is about to take a giant step forward.

KURT: Talking of that, do you know who it is who's writing those idiotic articles in the newspaper?

CAPTAIN [reddens]: I don't know, but why do you call them idiotic?

ALICE [to KURT]: Watch out. He wrote them.

KURT [to ALICE]: He? [To the CAPTAIN.] Perhaps I should have said not wholly informed.

CAPTAIN: You are not able to judge.

ALICE: Are you two trying to pick a quarrel?

KURT: No —

CAPTAIN: It's difficult to stay friends with anyone on this island, but we two should set an example —

KURT: Yes, can you explain that to me? When I first came here I soon got friendly with all the authorities, and became particularly intimate with the Judge Advocate — well, as intimate as one can, at our age. But after a while — I remember, it happened soon after you got well — they suddenly all began to act very coldly towards me, and yesterday the Judge Advocate cut me on the promenade. I was very upset. [*The* CAPTAIN *is silent.*] Have you noticed any unfriendliness towards you?

CAPTAIN: No, on the contrary.

ALICE [*to* KURT]: Don't you see, he's stolen your friends.

KURT [*to the* CAPTAIN]: I wondered if it could be that new share issue I refused to come in on?

CAPTAIN: Oh, I'm sure not. But can you tell me why you didn't want to subscribe?

KURT: Because I'd already invested my small savings in a lime works. And also, well, a new issue suggests that the old shares are shaky.

CAPTAIN [*absent-mindedly*]: That's a superb lamp you have. Where did you get it?

KURT: In town, of course.

ALICE [*to* KURT]: Watch out for your lamp, now.

KURT [*to the* CAPTAIN]: You mustn't think I'm ungrateful or disloyal, Edgar.

CAPTAIN: Well, it isn't very loyal of you to edge out of something you helped to start.

KURT: My dear Edgar, common prudence demands that one should try to save oneself and what one has while there is still time.

CAPTAIN: Save oneself? Is there some danger afoot? Is someone planning to rob you?

KURT: Why do you use such words?

CAPTAIN: Weren't you pleased when I helped you to invest your capital at six per cent?

KURT: Yes, I was very grateful.

CAPTAIN: You are not grateful now. Still, you're made that way and you can't help it.

ALICE [to KURT]: Listen to him!

KURT: Doubtless my character is imperfect and doubtless it sometimes gets the better of me, but I never deny my obligations —

CAPTAIN: Show it, then. [Reaches out a hand and takes a newspaper.] Hullo! What's this? An announcement — [Reads.] The Chief Medical Officer is dead. [as though to himself.] This will involve certain changes.

ALICE [to KURT]: He can't even wait till the fellow's buried.

KURT [to the CAPTAIN]: What kind of changes?

CAPTAIN [gets up]: No doubt we'll learn.

ALICE: Where are you going?

CAPTAIN: I think I must go into town. [Catches sight of a letter-card on the desk, registers it mentally, reads the outside of it and puts it back.] Forgive this digression.

KURT: Not at all.

CAPTAIN: Aren't those Allan's mathematical instruments? Where is the boy?

KURT: He's out playing with the girls.

CAPTAIN: That big lad? I don't like that. And Judith will have to watch herself. You must keep an eye on your young man. And I'll keep one on my young lady. [Walks *past the piano and strikes a few notes.*] Superb tone this instrument has. A Steinbech? Eh?

KURT: Bechstein.

CAPTAIN: You're doing well for yourself, Kurt. You should be grateful to me for bringing you here.

ALICE [*to* KURT]: He's lying. He tried to stop you coming.

CAPTAIN: Well, goodbye, you two. I'll catch the next boat. [*Goes, inspecting the paintings on the walls en route.*]

ALICE: Well?

KURT: Well?

ALICE: I still don't get what he's up to. But tell me one thing. That envelope he was looking at. Who's it from?

KURT: I must confess, that was my one secret.

ALICE: And he sniffed it out. He's a demon, I told you. Is the sender's name on the outside?

KURT: Yes. "Constituency Headquarters".

ALICE: Then he's guessed your secret. You're hoping to stand for Parliament. Now you'll see — he'll go for the candidacy and get it.

KURT: Has he ever had plans in that direction?

ALICE: No, but he has now. I saw it in his face while he was reading the envelope.

KURT: Is that why he's going into town?

ALICE: No. He decided that when he saw the obituary notice.

KURT: What can he gain from the Medical Officer's death?

ALICE: You tell me. Perhaps he was some enemy who stood in his way.

KURT: If he's as dreadful as you say, then one has reason to fear him.

ALICE: Didn't you hear how he wanted to steal you, to tie your hands by making you feel ungrateful without any reason at all? He never got you this job, he tried to stop you getting it. He's a stealer of souls, a parasite, a worm who wants to eat your entrails, so that one day you'll find yourself hollow like a rotten tree. He hates you, even though he's bound to you by the memory of your early friendship —

KURT: How penetrative one becomes when one hates someone.

ALICE: And blind when one loves. Blind and stupid.

KURT: Alice! Don't talk like that.

ALICE: Do you know what is meant by a vampire? It's the soul of a dead person that looks for a living body to dwell in as a parasite. Edgar is dead, ever since that day he fell. He has no interests, no personality, no initiative. But once he gets hold of someone he sinks his teeth into them, drops his roots into their flesh and starts to grow and bloom. Now he has fastened on to you.

KURT: If he comes too close I'll shake him off.

ALICE: Shake off a leech? Just you try. Do you know why he doesn't want Judith and Allan to meet?

KURT: I suppose he's afraid of them getting hurt.

ALICE: It's not that. He wants to marry Judith off — to the Colonel.

KURT [startled]: That old widower?

ALICE: Yes.

KURT: How horrible. What does she say?

ALICE: If she could get the General, who's eighty, she'd take him, to spite the Colonel, who's sixty. Spite, Kurt — that's what she lives on. Jackboots and spite — those are the only words that breed understands.

KURT: Judith? That beautiful young girl — so proud, so full of life?

ALICE: Yes. We know her. May I sit here and write a letter?

KURT [*tidies the desk*]: Of course.

ALICE [*takes off her gloves and sits at the desk*]: Now I'll try my hand as a tactician. I failed once, when I tried to kill that monster. But now I've learned the craft.

KURT: You know that one must load before one shoots?

ALICE: Yes. And with real bullets.

> KURT *goes out right.* ALICE *thinks and writes.*
> ALLAN *runs in without noticing her and throws himself headlong on the sofa, sobbing into a lace handkerchief.* ALICE *watches him for a moment, then gets up and goes over to the sofa.*

ALICE [*gently*]: Allan!

> ALLAN *sits up embarrassed, and hides the handkerchief behind his back.*

ALICE [*gentle, feminine, earnest*]: You mustn't be afraid of me, Allan. You have nothing to fear from me. What's the matter? Are you ill?

ALLAN: Yes.

ALICE: What's wrong with you?

ALLAN: I don't know.

ALICE: Have you a headache?

ALLAN: No.

ALICE [*touches her breast*]: Something here?

ALLAN: Yes.

ALICE: It hurts, so that your heart wants to break? And it tears, and tears —

ALLAN: How do you know that?

ALICE: And then one wants to die, one wishes one were
dead, and everything's so difficult. And one thinks only
of one thing — or rather, one person — but if two people
think about the same person, then one of those two is
doomed. [ALLAN *has forgotten himself and is picking at
his handkerchief.*] It's the sickness which no one can cure
— one can't eat, one doesn't want to drink, one only wants
to weep, and one weeps so bitterly. Preferably out in the
forest, so no one can see, because people laugh at that
kind of grief. People are cruel! Ugh! What do you want
from her? Nothing. You don't want to kiss her mouth,
because then you believe you would die. When your
thoughts fly to her, you feel as though death had touched
you. And it is death, my child. The death that gives life.
But you can't understand that yet. There's a smell of
violets. It is she! [*Approaches* ALLAN *and slowly takes
his handkerchief.*] It is she, she is everywhere, she and
only she. [*Laughs loudly.* ALLAN *hides his face in her
lap.*] Poor boy! Poor boy! Oh, how it hurts, how it hurts!
[*Dries his tears with the handkerchief.*] There, there,
there. Cry, cry, yes. It will ease your heart. [*Pause.*] But
now, get up, Allan, and be a man, otherwise she won't
want to look at you. The cruel one, who is not cruel. Has
she tormented you? With the Lieutenant? Listen, my boy.
You must be friends with the Lieutenant, then you'll be
able to talk about her together. That helps a little too.

ALLAN: I don't want to see the Lieutenant.

ALICE: Listen, little boy. It won't be long before the
Lieutenant comes to see you to talk about her. Because —
[ALLAN *looks up with a glimmer of hope.*] Well, shall I
be nice and tell you? [*He bows his head.*] Because he is
as unhappy as you.

ALLAN [*happily*]: No?

ALICE: Of course he is, and he needs someone to open his
heart to when Judith hurts him. You seem happy already!

ALLAN: Doesn't she want the Lieutenant?

ALICE: She doesn't want you either, my dear. She wants the Colonel. [*He is downcast again.*] Is it raining again? You can't keep that handkerchief, Judith minds about her belongings and won't like losing it. [*He looks crestfallen.*] Well, Allan, that's how Judith is. Sit there now while I write another letter, then you can go on an errand for me.

> *She goes to the desk and writes. The* LIEUTENANT *enters upstage. He looks melancholy without appearing comic. He does not notice* ALICE *but makes for* ALLAN.

LIEUTENANT: Cadet! [ALLAN *springs to attention.*] Please sit down.

> ALICE *watches them. The* LIEUTENANT *goes over to* ALLAN *and sits beside him. Sighs, takes out a handkerchief like the one we have seen and dries his forehead.* ALLAN *looks at the handkerchief covetously. The* LIEUTENANT *looks at* ALLAN *sadly.* ALICE *coughs. The* LIEUTENANT *springs to attention.*

ALICE: Please sit down.

LIEUTENANT: I beg your pardon, madam.

ALICE: Not at all. Please sit there and keep the cadet company. He feels a little lonely on this island. [*Writes.*]

LIEUTENANT [*softly to* ALLAN, *embarrassed*]: It's terribly hot.

ALLAN: Yes.

LIEUTENANT: Have you finished Book Six yet?

ALLAN: I'm just doing the last problem.

LIEUTENANT: That's a tricky one.

> *Silence.*

LIEUTENANT: Have you — [*searches for words*] — played tennis today?

ALLAN: No, it was too hot in the sun.

LIEUTENANT [*tormented, but not absurdly so*]: Yes, it's tremendously hot today.

ALLAN [*whispers*]: Yes, it is very hot.

   Silence.

LIEUTENANT: Have you — been out sailing today?

ALLAN: No, I couldn't get anyone to crew for me.

LIEUTENANT: Would you — trust me to — crew for you?

ALLAN [*respectfully, as before*]: It would be too great an honour, Lieutenant.

LIEUTENANT: By no means, by no means. Do you think — there'll be a good breeze today, around noon? That's the only time I can be free.

ALLAN [*shrewdly*]: There'll be very little wind at noon, and — that's when Miss Judith has her lesson —

LIEUTENANT [*crestfallen*]: I see, I see. Hm. Do you think that — ?

ALICE: Would one of you two young gentlemen be so kind as to take a letter for me? [*The two men look at each other distrustfully.*] To Miss Judith? [ALLAN *and the* LIEUTENANT *jump up and go over to* ALICE, *but with a certain dignity so as to conceal their feelings.*] Both of you? It'll be all the surer to reach her, then! [*Hands the letter to the* LIEUTENANT.] Oh, Lieutenant, may I have that handkerchief? My daughter gets so worried if she loses any of her clothes. She's rather small-minded about such things. Would you let me have it, please? I don't want to laugh, but you two really mustn't make yourselves ridiculous — unnecessarily. And the Colonel doesn't like to act Othello. [*Takes the handkerchief.*] Be off with you now, the pair of you, and try to hide your feelings as best you can!

   The LIEUTENANT *bows and goes, closely followed by* ALLAN.

ALICE [*calls*]: Allan!

ALLAN [*stops unwillingly in doorway*]: Yes, Aunt Alice?

ALICE: You'd better stay. If you don't want to hurt yourself more than you can bear.

ALLAN: But he's going!

ALICE: Let him burn his fingers. But you take care.

ALLAN: I don't want to take care.

ALICE: You'll cry later. And I'll have to be the one who'll comfort you.

ALLAN: I want to go!

ALICE: Go, then. But come back, you young idiot, so that I have the chance to laugh at you.

> ALLAN *runs after the* LIEUTENANT. ALICE *writes again.*

KURT [*enters*]: Alice, I've received an anonymous letter which bothers me.

ALICE: Have you noticed that ever since Edgar put away that uniform he's been another person? I never thought a coat could do so much.

KURT: You haven't answered my question.

ALICE: It wasn't a question, it was a statement. What are you frightened of?

KURT: Everything.

ALICE: He's going in to town. Those trips always have some unpleasant outcome.

KURT: But I can't take any measures, because I don't know from which point the attack will come.

ALICE [*seals her letter*]: Let's see if I've guessed right.

KURT: Will you help me, then?

ALICE: Yes. But no further than my interests allow. That is to say, my children's.

KURT: I understand. Listen — how quiet it is here, in the fields, on the sea, everywhere!

ALICE: But behind the silence I can hear voices — wailing, screaming.

KURT: Ssh! I hear something too. No, it was only the gulls.

ALICE: I can hear something else. Well, I'll go to the post-office. With this letter.

Scene 2

The same. ALLAN *is working at the desk.* JUDITH *is standing in the doorway in a tennis hat holding the handlebars of a bicycle.*

JUDITH: Can I borrow your screwdriver?

ALLAN [*not looking up*]: No, you can't.

JUDITH: You're being rude now, every time I ask you for something.

ALLAN [*not harshly*]: I'm not being anything, I just want to be left in peace.

JUDITH [*comes forward*]: Allan.

ALLAN: Well, what is it?

JUDITH: You mustn't be angry with me.

ALLAN: I'm not.

JUDITH: Give me your hand on it.

ALLAN [*gently*]: I don't want to take your hand, but I'm not angry. What do you want with me, really?

JUDITH: Oh, you're so stupid!

ALLAN: If you say so.

JUDITH: You think I'm just nasty.

ALLAN: No, I know you're kind too. You *can* be kind.

JUDITH: Well, it's not my fault that you and the Lieutenant go off and cry together. Tell me, why do you cry? [ALLAN *is embarrassed.*] Tell me. I never cry. And why are you such good friends now? What do you talk about as you walk arm in arm? [*He does not answer.*] Allan! You'll soon see what I really am, and that I can do things for those I care about. And I'll give you one piece of advice — though I don't want to tell tales. You watch out —

ALLAN: For what?

JUDITH: Unpleasantnesses.

ALLAN: From whom?

JUDITH: From the direction you least expect.

ALLAN: I'm pretty used to unpleasantnesses. I haven't had so much fun out of life. What's brewing now?

JUDITH [*thoughtfully*]: You poor boy. Give me your hand! [*He stretches out his hand.*] Look at me. Daren't you look at me?

   He runs out left to hide his emotion.

LIEUTENANT [*enters upstage*]: Excuse me. I was hoping to find Cadet —

JUDITH: Tell me, Lieutenant. Do you want to be my friend? May I confide in you?

LIEUTENANT: If you choose so to honour me —

JUDITH: I do. Just one word. Don't abandon Allan, when it happens.

LIEUTENANT: When what happens?

JUDITH: You'll soon see — perhaps today. Do you like Allan?

LIEUTENANT: The young man is my best pupil, and I

admire him also for his strength of character. There are
moments in life when one needs — [*stresses the words*]
— strength to — in a word, to carry on, to endure, to
suffer.

JUDITH: That's more than one word. But — you like Allan?

LIEUTENANT: Yes.

JUDITH: Go and find him, and stay with him —

LIEUTENANT: That was why I came here. I had no other
motive —

JUDITH: I wasn't suggesting you had. Of the kind you
mean. Allan went out that way. [*Points left.*]

LIEUTENANT [*as he hesitantly exists left*]: I — I will do
as you suggest.

JUDITH: Please do.

ALICE [*enters upstage*]: What are you doing here?

JUDITH: I wanted to borrow a screwdriver.

ALICE: Will you listen to me for a moment?

JUDITH: Certainly. [ALICE *sits on the sofa.* JUDITH
remains standing.] But say what you have to say quickly.
I don't like long lectures.

ALICE: Don't you? Right. Put up your hair and wear a
long dress.

JUDITH: Why?

ALICE: Because you're not a child any longer. And you're
too young to need to act as though you were younger.

JUDITH: What does that mean?

ALICE: That you're old enough for marriage, and that the
way you dress now causes offence.

JUDITH: All right. I will.

ALICE: You understand, then?

JUDITH: Oh, yes.

ALICE: And we're agreed?

JUDITH: Completely.

ALICE: On all points?

JUDITH: Every one.

ALICE: Will you also please stop playing — with Allan?

JUDITH: You want me to be serious?

ALICE: Yes.

JUDITH: Then we can start at once.

She has put down her bicycle handlebars and now lets down her cycling-skirt, reshapes her plait into a bun, takes a hairpin from her mother's hair and fastens her own.

ALICE: One doesn't perform one's toilet in other people's houses.

JUDITH: Am I all right like this? Right, I'm ready. Now, come who dares!

ALICE: Well, at least you look respectable now. And leave Allan in peace.

JUDITH: I don't know what you mean by that.

ALICE: Can't you see he's suffering?

JUDITH: Yes, I think I noticed. But I can't imagine why. I'm not suffering.

ALICE: That's *your* strength. But you wait. One day — oh, yes, you'll know. Go home now, and don't forget you have a long dress on.

JUDITH: Must one walk differently, too?

ALICE: Try.

JUDITH [*tries to walk like a lady*]: Oh! It's like wearing clogs, my feet are tied, I can't run any more!

ALICE: Yes, child. Now you must learn to walk, the slow road towards the unknown, which one knows about but must pretend to know nothing of. Shorter steps — and slower, much slower! You must throw away your children's shoes and start wearing boots, Judith. You don't remember when you gave up oversocks and started wearing shoes, but I remember.

JUDITH: I shall never be able to stand this!

ALICE: But you must. You must!

JUDITH [*goes to her mother and kisses her lightly on the forehead, then exits gravely like a lady, forgetting her handlebars*]: Goodbye!

KURT [*enters right*]: Are you here already?

ALICE: Yes.

KURT: Has *he* been here again?

ALICE: Yes.

KURT: What was he wearing?

ALICE: The lot. So he must have been to see the Colonel. Two medals on his chest!

KURT: Two? I knew he'd get one when he retired. What's the other?

ALICE: I don't know what it was. A white cross inside a red one.

KURT: Must have been Portuguese, then. Wait a minute. Let me think. Those magazine articles of his, weren't they about quarantine conditions in Portuguese ports.

ALICE: As far as I remember, yes.

KURT: And he has never been in Portugal?

ALICE: Never.

KURT: I have, though.

ALICE: Why tell me this? He can hear, and has a good memory.

KURT: Don't you think Judith must have got him that decoration?

ALICE: Now really! There are limits. [Gets up.] And you have overstepped them.

KURT: Are we going to quarrel now?

ALICE: Depends on you. Keep your nose out of my affairs.

KURT: When they touch mine, I can't ignore them. Here he comes.

ALICE: Now it will happen.

KURT: What will happen?

ALICE: We shall see.

KURT: Let's hope he comes into the open. I can't stand this state of siege much longer. I haven't a friend left on the whole island.

ALICE: Wait. Sit here on the sofa. He'll take the armchair. Don't worry, I'll prompt you.

CAPTAIN [enters upstage in full dress uniform wearing the Order of the Sword and the Portuguese Order of Christ]: Good morning! So. We meet.

ALICE: You're tired. Sit down. [The CAPTAIN sits unexpectedly on the left side of the sofa.] Make yourself comfortable.

CAPTAIN: I'm happy here. You are too kind.

ALICE [to KURT]: Be careful, he suspects us.

CAPTAIN [irritably]: What did you say?

ALICE [to KURT]: He must have been drinking.

CAPTAIN [roughly]: No, he hasn't been.

Silence.

CAPTAIN: Well. How have you two been amusing yourselves?

ALICE: How have you?

CAPTAIN: Are you looking at my medals?

ALICE: No.

CAPTAIN: I think you are. You're envious. People nor-
mally congratulate one on receiving a decoration.

ALICE: Congratulations.

CAPTAIN: We get these things the way actresses get laurel
wreaths.

ALICE: If you're referring to the ones on the walls at
hóme —

CAPTIAN: Which you got from your brother —

ALICE: Oh, shut up.

CAPTAIN: And before which I have had to genuflect for
twenty-five years. And which took me twenty-five years
to learn the truth about.

ALICE: Have you met my brother?

CAPTAIN: Yes.

    ALICE *is crushed. Silence.*

CAPTAIN: Well, Kurt. You're saying nothing, old chap.

KURT: I'm waiting.

CAPTAIN: By the way. You've heard the big news?

KURT: No.

CAPTAIN: Well, it's not pleasant for me to have to be the
one who tells you —

KURT: What is it?

CAPTAIN: The lime works has gone bust.

KURT: That is bad news. How does it affect you?

CAPTAIN: I'm all right. I sold in time.

KURT: How clever of you.

CAPTAIN: But how does it affect you?

KURT: Badly.

CAPTAIN: It's your own fault. You should either have sold in time or subscribed to those new shares.

KURT: Then I'd have lost them too.

CAPTAIN: No. Then the company would have stayed solvent.

KURT: Not the company, only the board. In my opinion that new issue was just a whip-round for the directors.

CAPTAIN: Will this opinion save you? Ask yourself.

KURT: No. I shall lose everything.

CAPTAIN: Everything.

KURT: Even my house and furniture.

CAPTAIN: How terrible.

KURT: I've known worse.

   Silence.

CAPTAIN: That's what happens when amateurs speculate.

KURT: You surprise me. You know that if I hadn't subscribed, I'd have been boycotted. New opportunities for local industry, unlimited capital, unlimited as the ocean, philanthropy, national asset — that's what you wrote about it, and got printed. And now you call it speculation?

CAPTAIN [*unmoved*]: What do you plan to do now?

KURT: I shall have to auction everything I have.

CAPTAIN: Yes, you'd better.

KURT: What do you mean by that?

CAPTAIN: What I said. [*Slowly.*] Certain changes are going to take place here —

KURT: On this island, you mean?

CAPTAIN: Yes. For example — you will have to exchange your present abode for a humbler one.

KURT: I see.

CAPTAIN: Yes, the idea is to move the quarantine station to the coast, so that it will be next to the water.

KURT: But that was my original idea!

CAPTAIN [*drily*]: I don't know about that. I am not aware of your views on the subject. However — I think you would be wise to dispose of your furniture now so that it will attract less attention. The scandal, I mean.

KURT: What?

CAPTAIN: The scandal. [*Works himself up.*] For it is a scandal to come to a new place and immediately start speculating in a manner calculated to cause the maximum embarrassment to one's blood relations.

KURT: Surely I shall be the one who will suffer most embarrassment.

CAPTAIN: I must tell you something, my dear Kurt. If you hadn't had me on your side in this crisis, you'd have lost your job.

KURT: That too!

CAPTAIN: You don't always seem able to behave like a gentleman. There have been complaints about you.

KURT: Justifiable complaints?

CAPTAIN: Yes! For you are — despite your other admirable qualities — a slop. Don't interrupt me. You are a dreadful slop.

KURT: You surprise me.

CAPTAIN: However. I think it would be wise for you to move as soon as possible. And I would advise you to arrange that auction immediately, or better still try to sell the stuff privately.

KURT: Privately? Where will I find a purchaser here?

CAPTAIN: Surely you are not implying that I would wish to sit in your chairs? That would be a pretty thing — [*Begins to speak in bursts.*] Hm! Especially if one—remembers what happened — in the past —

KURT: What was that? You mean what *didn't* happen —

CAPTAIN [*changes tack*]: Alice is very quiet. What's the matter, old lady? Have you become a vegetable?

ALICE: I'm thinking.

CAPTAIN: Oh, God! Are you thinking? Well, you must think quickly and sharply, and precisely, if it's to be any use. Right, now, think! One, two, three! [*Roars with laughter.*] Can't you? Well then, I'll go. Where is Judith?

ALICE: She's somewhere.

CAPTAIN: Where is Allan? [ALICE *is silent.*] Where is the Lieutenant? [ALICE *is silent.*] Tell me, Kurt. What are you thinking of doing with Allan now?

KURT: Doing with him?

CAPTAIN: Yes, you won't be able to afford to keep him in the Artillery, will you?

KURT: Perhaps not.

CAPTAIN: You must try to get him into some cheap infantry regiment, up in Lapland or somewhere.

KURT: Lapland?

CAPTAIN: Yes. Unless you put him into some trade. If I were you I'd start him in some office — Why not? [KURT *is silent.*] In these enlightened times! Yes. How extraordinarily silent you are, Alice. Well, my children, such is life's seesaw, one moment one's up aloft as cocky as you please, the next moment one's down, and then up one pops again. Etcetera! So much for that. Yes. [*To* ALICE.] Did you say something? [*She shakes her head.*] We can expect company here within the next few days.

ALICE: Did you say something to me?

CAPTAIN: We can expect company within the next few days. Important company.

ALICE: Who?

CAPTAIN: You see. You're interested. Now you can sit down and guess who they'll be, and between guesses you can read this letter once again. [*Hands her an open letter.*]

ALICE: My letter! Opened. Which I sent to the post-office?

CAPTAIN [*gets up*]: Yes. In my capacity as head of the family and your legal guardian I protect the sacred interests of that family and block with an iron hand any attempt to loosen the ties of blood by criminal correspondence! So! [ALICE *is crushed.*] I am not dead, Alice, but you must not get angry at my trying to extricate us all from this unmerited humiliation. Unmerited by me, at any rate.

ALICE: Judith! Judith!

CAPTAIN: Am I to be her Holofernes? Pah! [*Goes out upstage.*]

KURT: Who is this man?

ALICE: Don't ask me.

KURT: We're beaten.

ALICE: Beyond doubt.

KURT: He has gnawed me to pieces, but so cunningly that I can't accuse him of anything.

ALICE: On the contrary. You are in his debt.

KURT: Does he know what he's doing?

ALICE: No, I don't think so. He follows his nature and his instincts. And just now he seems to be in favour with the powers that dispense good and evil.

KURT: I suppose it must be the Colonel he's expecting.

ALICE: Must be. That's why he wants Allan out of the way.

KURT: And you agree with him?

ALICE: Yes.

KURT: Then our ways must part.

ALICE: A little. But we shall meet again.

KURT: Probably.

ALICE: And you know where.

KURT: Here.

ALICE: You feel that?

KURT: It's obvious. He will take my home, and buy my furniture.

ALICE: I think so too. But don't abandon me.

KURT: Not for so little.

ALICE: Goodbye. [*Goes.*]

KURT: Goodbye.

Scene 3

The same. Outside it is overcast and raining. ALICE *and* KURT *enter upstage in raincoats with umbrellas.*

ALICE: Well, I've got you here! Kurt, I won't be so cruel as to say "Welcome" to your old home.

KURT: Oh! Why? I've gone through this three times in my life — and more besides. It doesn't bother me.

ALICE: Did he summon you here?

KURT: It was a formal summons. I don't know on what grounds.

ALICE: He isn't your boss, is he?

KURT: No. But he's established himself as King of this island. And as soon as anyone resists he mentions the Colonel's name and everyone touches their forelock. By the way, is it today that the Colonel's coming?

ALICE: He's expected, but I don't know for sure. Sit down.

KURT [sits]: Everything's the same here.

ALICE: Don't think about it. Don't open the wound.

KURT: Wound? I just think it's a little strange. Strange like that man. Do you know, when I first met him as a young man, I ran away from him. But he came after me. Flattered me, offered me his services, and bound me to him. I tried to run away again, but it was useless. Now I am his slave.

ALICE: Yes, why? He's really in your debt, but you're the one who suffers.

KURT: Since I became ruined, he has offered to help Allan through his exam —

ALICE: You'll have to pay dearly for it. That candidature of yours for Parliament — is that still on?

KURT: Yes — as far as I can see, there should be no obstacle.

   Silence.

ALICE: Is Allan really leaving today?

KURT: Yes. If I can't stop him.

ALICE: That was a short happiness for you.

KURT: Short like everything else, except life, which is horribly long.

ALICE: Yes. Won't you go inside and wait in the drawing-room? If this place doesn't upset you it does me.

KURT: If you want me to.

ALICE: I'm ashamed, I'm ashamed to death. But I can't change it.

KURT: Let's go, then. As you wish.

ALICE: Someone's coming, anyway.

They go into the room left. The CAPTAIN *and* ALLAN *enter upstage, both in uniform with military caps.*

CAPTAIN: Sit down here, my boy, I want to talk with you. [*Sits in arm chair.* ALLAN *sits in the chair left.*] It's raining today. When it's fine I like to sit here and look at the sea. [*Silence.*] Well? You don't want to go, then?

ALLAN: I don't want to leave my father.

CAPTAIN: Ah, yes, your father. He is a rather unfortunate man. [*Silence.*] And parents seldom understand what is best for their children. That is — naturally there are exceptions. Hm! Tell me, Allan. Have you any contact with your mother?

ALLAN: Yes, she writes sometimes.

CAPTAIN: You know that she is your legal guardian?

ALLAN: Yes.

CAPTAIN: Tell me, Allan. Are you aware that your mother has given me a power of attorney to take decisions on her behalf?

ALLAN: I didn't know that.

CAPTAIN: Well, you know now. So there will be no further discussion of what you will do. You will go to Lapland.

ALLAN: But I haven't the money.

CAPTAIN: I have seen to that.

ALLAN: Then I have nothing left but to thank you, Uncle.

CAPTAIN: You're a grateful lad. Not everyone is. Hm! [*Raises his voice.*] The Colonel — do you know the Colonel?

ALLAN [*embarrassed*]: No, I don't.

CAPTAIN: The Colonel — [*underlines his words*] — is a close personal friend of mine — [*more quickly*] — as perhaps you know. The Colonel has chosen to take an interest in my family, including my wife's relatives. The Colonel has by his personal intervention succeeded in obtaining for you the money required for you to complete your training. Now you know your debt and your father's debt to the Colonel. Have I made myself clear? [ALLAN *bows.*] Go now and pack your things. The money will be handed to you when you go on board. Well, goodbye, my boy.

> *He gets up and goes out right.* ALLAN, *dejected, looks round the room.* JUDITH *enters upstage with an umbrella, wearing a hood. Beneath this she is elegantly dressed, with a long skirt and her hair up.*

JUDITH: Is that Allan?

ALLAN [*turns and looks at her closely*]: Is *that* Judith?

JUDITH: You don't recognize me? But where have you been for so long? What are you looking at? My long dress — and my hair? You haven't seen it like that before?

ALLAN: No.

JUDITH: Do I look like a woman?

> *He turns away.*

JUDITH [*earnestly*]: What are you doing here?

ALLAN: I've resigned my post.

JUDITH: What? Are you going away?

ALLAN: I am being sent to Lapland.

JUDITH [*shocked*]: To Lapland? When will you leave?

ALLAN: Today.

JUDITH: Whose idea is that?

ALLAN: Your father's.

JUDITH: I might have guessed. [*Walks a few paces and stamps her foot.*] I wish you could have stayed today.

ALLAN: To meet the Colonel?

JUDITH: What do you know about the Colonel? Must you go?

ALLAN: I have no choice. And now I want to.

    Silence.

JUDITH: Why do you want to now?

ALLAN: I want to get away from here. Out into the world.

JUDITH: It's too confined here! Yes, I understand you, Allan. It's intolerable here. They speculate. In lime, and in human beings.

    Silence.

JUDITH [*sincerely*]: Allan. You know me. I'm happy, I don't easily suffer. But now I'm beginning to learn.

ALLAN: You?

JUDITH: Yes. Now I'm beginning. [*Presses both hands against her breast.*] Oh, how it hurts! Oh!

ALLAN: What is it?

JUDITH: I don't know. I'm — choking. I think I'm dying.

ALLAN: Judith!

JUDITH [*screams*]: Ah! Is *this* how it feels? Like this? You poor boys!

ALLAN: I ought to laugh, if I were as cruel as you.

JUDITH: I'm not cruel. I just didn't know any better. You mustn't go.

ALLAN: I must.

JUDITH: Go, then. But give me a remembrance.

ALLAN: What have I to give you?

JUDITH [in genuine agony]: Allan! No, I won't let this happen! [Screams and clutches her breast.] I'm suffering, I'm suffering! What have you done to me? I don't want to live any more. Allan, don't go, not alone. We'll go together, we'll take the little dinghy, the little white one — and we'll sail out together, under full sail — there's a good wind — and we'll sink, out there, far out where there's no snare-grass, no jellyfish — ! Well? Say something! But we should have washed the sails yesterday — they ought to be pure white — I want to see white at that moment — and then you'll swim with me in your arms until you tire — and then we'll sink — ! [Turns.] That's beautiful. Much more beautiful than to sit here and grieve, writing secret letters which Father will open and laugh at. Allan! [Takes his arms and shakes him.] Are you listening?

ALLAN [who has been watching her with shining eyes]: Judith! Judith! Why didn't you say this before?

JUDITH: Because I didn't know how to say it. I didn't know.

ALLAN: And now I have to leave you! But I suppose it's the best way — the only way. I can't compete with a man who —

JUDITH: Don't speak of the Colonel.

ALLAN: Isn't it true?

JUDITH: It is true — and untrue.

ALLAN: Could it become quite untrue?

JUDITH: Yes. Now it shall. Within an hour.

ALLAN: Will you promise me that? I can wait, I can suffer, I can work. Judith!

JUDITH: Don't go yet. How long must I wait?

ALLAN: A year.

JUDITH [*joyfully*]: A year? I shall wait a thousand years, and if you don't come then I shall spin the sky backwards so that the sun will rise in the west! Hush, someone's coming. Allan, we must part! Hush. Hold me tightly! [*They embrace.*] But you mustn't kiss me. [*Turns away her head.*] No — go now! Go now!

> ALLAN *goes upstage and puts on his cloak. Then they run into each other's arms so that* JUDITH *disappears inside the cloak and they kiss for a moment.* ALLAN *runs out.* JUDITH *throws herself on the sofa and sobs.* ALLAN *comes back and falls on his knees by the sofa.*

ALLAN: No, I can't go! I can't leave you now!

JUDITH [*gets up*]: If you knew how beautiful you are now, if you could see yourself!

ALLAN: Ssh! A man can't be beautiful! But you, Judith! You — that *you* — I see now that when you were kind, another Judith appeared. That one is mine. But if you fail me, I shall die.

JUDITH: I think I shall die anyway! Oh, if I could die now, when I am happy!

ALLAN: Someone's coming!

JUDITH: Let them come! I'm not afraid of anything in the whole world now! But I wish you'd take me under your cloak. [*She pretends to hide beneath it.*] And that I could run away with you to Lapland! What shall we do in Lapland? Join that regiment that has plumes in its hats? That's a handsome uniform, it will suit you well. [*Fondles his hair. He kisses her finger-tips, one after the other, then kisses her boot.*] What are you doing, you young lunatic?

Your face'll get black. [*Gets up violently.*] And then I
won't be able to kiss you when you go. Come! I'll go with
you.

ALLAN: No, you mustn't. I'll be arrested.

JUDITH: I'll be arrested with you.

ALLAN: You couldn't. No, we must part.

JUDITH: I'll swim after the steamer — then you'll jump
overboard and save me, and it'll be in the paper, and
we'll get engaged! Shall we do that?

ALLAN: You can still joke about this?

JUDITH: It's always easy to weep. Say goodbye now!

> *They embrace passionately, then* ALLAN *runs out
> through the door upstage. It remains open. They
> embrace again outside in the rain.*

ALLAN: You'll get soaked. Judith!

JUDITH: What do I care?

> *They tear themselves apart.* ALLAN *goes.*
> JUDITH *stands in the rain and wind which blows
> her hair and clothes while she waves her hand-
> kerchief. Then she runs inside and throws herself
> on the sofa, her face in her hands.*

ALICE [*enters and goes over to* JUDITH]: What's the
matter? Are you ill? Stand up and let me look at you.
[JUDITH *gets up.* ALICE *looks at her closely.*] No,
you aren't ill. But I can't comfort you.

> *She goes out right. The* LIEUTENANT *enters upstage.*

JUDITH [*gets up and puts on her hooded cloak*]: Will you
accompany me to the telegraph-office, please, Lieutenant?

LIEUTENANT: Any way in which I can be of service —
but I doubt if it would seem proper —

JUDITH: So much the better! I want you to compromise me.
But don't get any illusions! You go first.

They go out upstage. The CAPTAIN *and* ALICE
enter right, the CAPTAIN *in undress uniform.*

CAPTAIN [*sits in the armchair*] : Let him in.

ALICE *goes left and opens the door, then sits on the
sofa.* KURT *enters left.*

KURT: You want to speak to me?

CAPTAIN [*amiably but somewhat condescendingly*] : Yes, I
have several important pieces of information to impart to
you. Sit down.

KURT [*sits on the chair left*] : I'm all ears.

CAPTAIN: Well. [*Oratorically.*] You are aware that the
subject of quarantine has been neglected in this country
for the best part of a century — hm!

ALICE [*to* KURT] : He's practising for Parliament.

CAPTAIN: But thanks to the unprecedented developments
now taking place in —

ALICE [*to* KURT] : Communications, of course.

CAPTAIN: — in every possible field, the Government has
decided to encourage further research. To this end the
Department of Health has appointed an inspector — and —

ALICE [*to* KURT] : He's dictating.

CAPTAIN: You may as well know now as later. I have
been appointed Inspector of Quarantine.

Silence.

KURT: May I congratulate you. And at the same time
formally pay my respects.

CAPTAIN: In view of the ties of blood that bind us, our
personal relationship will remain unchanged. Now, to
turn to other matters. Your son Allan has, at my request,
been transferred to an infantry regiment in Lapland.

KURT: But I don't want that.

CAPTAIN: In this matter your wishes take second place to those of the boy's mother. And the mother having granted me full legal authority to decide the boy's future, I have decided!

KURT: I admire you.

CAPTAIN: Is that your only reaction to being parted from your son? Have you no human feelings?

KURT: You mean I ought to be suffering?

CAPTAIN: Yes.

KURT: It would make you happy if I suffered. You want me to suffer?

CAPTAIN: Can you suffer, Kurt? There was a time once when I fell sick. You were present, and I can only recall that your face expressed undisguised joy.

ALICE: That's not true. Kurt sat by your bedside all night and calmed you when your conscience began to torment you. But once you had recovered, you showed him no gratitude —

CAPTAIN [pretending not to hear her]: So, Allan must leave us.

KURT: Who will find the money?

CAPTAIN: I have already done that — that is to say, we have. A consortium interested in the young man's future —

KURT: Consortium!

CAPTAIN: Yes. And that you may rest assured that the formalities have been observed, here are the lists. [Hands him some papers.]

KURT: Lists? [Studies them.] But these are charity lists!

CAPTAIN: You could call them that.

KURT: Have you been begging for my son?

CAPTAIN: Are you being ungrateful again? An ungrateful friend is the worst thing a man can have.

KURT: But this will ruin my credit as a citizen! And will mean the end of my candidature —

CAPTAIN: What candidature?

KURT: For Parliament, of course.

CAPTAIN: Surely you weren't seriously dreaming of that? Especially since I, as you might have guessed, have decided as the senior authority here to stand myself. You seem to have underrated me.

KURT: Well! So that's finished. That too.

CAPTAIN: It doesn't seem to bother you very greatly.

KURT: Now you have taken everything. Do you want anything more?

CAPTAIN: Have you anything more? And have you any grounds with which to reproach me? Think carefully, if you have any grounds with which to reproach me.

    Silence.

KURT: Strictly speaking, none. Everything has been done legally and correctly, like an everyday transaction between honourable fellow-citizens —

CAPTAIN: You speak with a resignation which strikes me as cynical. But your whole nature, my dear Kurt, is inclined towards cynicism, and there are moments when I am tempted to share Alice's opinion of you, that you are a hypocrite, a copper-bottomed hypocrite.

KURT [*calmly*]: Is that Alice's opinion?

ALICE [*to* KURT]: It was once. But not any longer. To endure what you have endured requires pure courage, or — something else.

CAPTAIN: Well, I think we can regard this discussion as closed. Be off now, Kurt, and say goodbye to Allan. He will leave by the next boat.

KURT [*gets up*]: So soon? Well. I have been through worse than this.

CAPTAIN: Yes, you say that so often. I begin to wonder what you got up to in America.

KURT: Got up to? Well, I encountered misfortune. And it's every human being's indisputable right to be smitten by misfortune.

CAPTAIN [*sharply*]: There are misfortunes that one brings upon oneself. Was yours that kind?

KURT: It was a question of conscience.

CAPTAIN [*curtly*]: Have you a conscience?

KURT: There are wolves and there are sheep, and it's no honour to be a sheep. But I'd rather be that than a wolf.

CAPTAIN: Don't you know the old saying, that every man creates his own luck?

KURT: Is *that* a saying?

CAPTAIN: And you should know that a man's strength —

KURT: Yes, I learned that that night when your strength failed you and you lay on the floor.

CAPTAIN [*raises his voice*]: A deserving person such as myself — yes, look at me! — I have fought for fifty years — against the world — and in the end I won, thanks to my steadfastness, my devotion to duty, my energy and — my sense of honour!

ALICE: You should let other people say that.

CAPTAIN: Other people don't say it because they are jealous of me. However! I am expecting a visitor. My daughter, Judith, is today to meet her future ... Where is Judith?

ALICE: She's out.

CAPTAIN: In this rain? Send for her.

KURT: Perhaps I may go now?

CAPTAIN: No, wait. Is Judith dressed? Properly?

ALICE: Well enough. Did the Colonel definitely say he'd come?

CAPTAIN [gets up]: Yes. That is — he wants to pay her a surprise visit, as the saying goes. And I expect his telegram any moment. [As he goes out right.] I shall be back shortly.

ALICE: What a man! Is he a man?

KURT: When you asked me that before, I answered no. Now I think him the most typical human being I could ever meet on this earth. Perhaps we're a little like him? Using people and exploiting opportunities?

ALICE: He has eaten you and your son alive. And you defend him?

KURT: I have known worse. This cannibal has left my soul untouched. He couldn't devour that.

ALICE: What "worse" have you known?

KURT: You ask that?

ALICE: Are you being discourteous?

KURT: I don't want to be. So — don't ask me again.

CAPTAIN [enters right]: The telegram was here all the time. Please read it to me, Alice, my eyes aren't so good. [Sits importantly in the armchair.] Read! Kurt need not leave us.

    ALICE glances through it quickly and silently, and looks astounded.

CAPTAIN: Well? Does it displease you?

    She looks at him silently.

CAPTAIN [sarcastically]: Who is it from?

ALICE: It is from the Colonel.

CAPTAIN [pleased]: I thought as much. Well, what does the Colonel say?

ALICE: He says this. "In view of Miss Judith's impertinent telephone message I consider our relationship terminated." [*Looks at the* CAPTAIN.]

CAPTAIN: Once more. If you please.

ALICE: "In view of Miss Judith's impertinent telephone message I consider our relationship terminated."

CAPTAIN [*pales*]: Judith!

ALICE: And Holofernes!

CAPTAIN: What are you, then?

ALICE: You'll soon see.

CAPTAIN: You have done this!

ALICE: No.

CAPTAIN [*wild with rage*]: You have done this!

ALICE: No!

> The CAPTAIN *tries to rise and draw his sabre, but collapses with a stroke.*

ALICE: Now you have your deserts!

CAPTAIN [*with an old man's tearfulness in his voice*]: Don't be angry with me! I'm so ill.

ALICE: Are you? I'm happy to hear it.

KURT: Let us carry him to his bed.

ALICE: No. I don't want to touch him. [*Rings the bell.*]

CAPTAIN [*as before*]: Alice — Kurt — you mustn't be angry with me. [*To* KURT]. Think of my children.

KURT: That's sublime. I'm to feel sorry for his children, when he has stolen mine!

ALICE: How can a man be so blind to himself?

CAPTAIN: Think of my children! [*He continues to slobber unintelligibly: "blu-blu-blu-blu".*]

ALICE: At last this tongue has stopped. It can brag no
longer, lie no longer, wound no longer. You, Kurt, who
believe in God! Thank Him from me! Thank Him for
freeing me from my prison, my wolf, my vampire!

KURT: Alice, don't talk like that.

ALICE [*puts her own face close to the* CAPTAIN's] : Where
is your "own strength" now? Well? And your "energy"?
[*He speechlessly spits in her face.*] Can you still spit
venom, viper? I'll tear the tongue from your mouth!
[*Strikes him in the face.*] The head is off but the cheek
still flushes, the blood still flows! Oh, Judith, my
darling girl, whom I carried like a vengeance beneath my
heart — you, you, have liberated us all! Have you more
heads, Hydra? We'll take them too! [*Seizes his beard.*]
So there *is* justice in the world! I dreamed it sometimes,
but never believed it. Kurt, ask God to forgive me for
misjudging Him! Oh, there *is* justice! Now I'll be one of
His lambs like you. Tell Him that, Kurt! A smile from
fortune makes us believers, unbroken adversity makes
us wolves.

     The LIEUTENANT *enters upstage.*

ALICE: The Captain has had a stroke. Help us, please.
Wheel his chair out.

LIEUTENANT: Madam —

ALICE: What is it?

LIEUTENANT: Miss Judith —

ALICE: Help us with this first. You can tell us about her
later. [*The* LIEUTENANT *wheels the chair out right.*]
Out with the corpse! Out with it, and open the doors!
Let's clean the air in here! [*Throws open the upstage
doors. The weather is now clear outside.*] Usch!

KURT: Are you going to abandon him?

ALICE: You abandon a wrecked ship, don't you? And the
crew save themselves. Why should I lay out the corpse of

a rotting beast? Let the scavengers or the anatomists have him! A garden would be too good a resting-place for this barrowload of muck. I'll go and wash myself all over, to cleanse my body of his touch, his filth. If I ever can.

> JUDITH *appears outside by the balustrade, bare-headed, waving her handkerchief towards the sea.*

KURT: Who's there? Judith! [*Shouts.*] Judith!

JUDITH [*enters, cries*]: He's gone!

KURT: Who?

JUDITH: Allan has gone.

KURT: Without saying goodbye?

JUDITH: We said goodbye. And he sends you his love, Uncle.

ALICE: So that was it!

JUDITH [*throws herself into* KURT's *arms*]: He's gone!

KURT: He will come back, dear child.

ALICE: Or we will follow him.

KURT [*with a gesture towards the door left*]: And leave *him*? The world —

ALICE: To hell with the world. Pah! Judith, come here to me. [JUDITH *goes over to her.* ALICE *kisses her on the forehead.*] Do you want to follow him?

JUDITH: Can you ask me?

ALICE: But your father is ill.

JUDITH: What do I care about that?

ALICE: That's my Judith! Oh, I love you! Judith!

JUDITH: Anyway, Father isn't small-minded, he hates sentimentality. He's a real aristocrat, Father, isn't he?

ALICE: In his way.

JUDITH: And I don't think he'll want to see me, after that telephone call I made. Well, why should he try to saddle me with some old man? No, Allan, Allan! [*Throws herself into* KURT's *arms.*] I want to go to Allan! [*Tears herself free and runs outside to wave.* KURT *follows her and waves too.*]

ALICE: Strange how flowers can blossom out of filth.

   The LIEUTENANT *enters right.*

ALICE: Yes?

LIEUTENANT: Madam — Miss Judith —

ALICE: Are you so impatient to speak her name that you forget the dying?

LIEUTENANT: But, Madam, she said —

ALICE: She? No, you'd better say Judith. But tell me first — how are things in there?

LIEUTENANT: In there? Yes — it's finished.

ALICE: Finished? Oh, God, I thank Thee, for my sake and all mankind's, that Thou hast freed us from this evil. Give me your arm, Kurt. I want to go outside and breathe. Breathe! [*The* LIEUTENANT *offers her his arm. She pauses.*] Did he say anything before he died?

LIEUTENANT: Miss Judith's father did say a few words.

ALICE: What did he say?

LIEUTENANT: He said: "Forgive them, for they know not what they do."

ALICE: Strange.

LIEUTENANT: Miss Judith's father was a good and noble man.

ALICE: Kurt!

   KURT *enters.*

ALICE: It is finished.

KURT: Ah!

ALICE: Do you know what his last words were? No, you don't. "Forgive them for they know not what they do."

KURT: Can you interpret that?

ALICE: I suppose he must have meant that *he* had always acted correctly, and that life had wronged him.

KURT: No doubt there'll be fine words spoken over his grave.

ALICE: And hundreds of wreaths. From his lieutenants.

KURT: Yes.

ALICE: A year ago he said, "It looks as though life is simply a gigantic fraud."

KURT: Do you think he was mocking us even at the moment of death?

ALICE: No. But now he's dead, I feel a curious urge to speak well of him.

KURT: Let us do that.

LIEUTENANT: Miss Judith's father was a good and noble man.

ALICE [to KURT]: You hear?

KURT: "They know not what they do." How often haven't I asked you that — if he knew what he was doing. And you didn't think he did. So forgive him.

ALICE: Riddles! Riddles! But listen. There is peace in this house now. The wonderful peace of death. As wonderful as the solemn unrest when a child is born into the world. I hear the silence — and I see the marks in the floor of the chair that carried him away. And I feel — that now my life is finished and I await corruption. You know, it's strange. Those simple words of the Lieutenant — and he is a simple soul — haunt me — but he is right. My husband, the love of my youth — yes, laugh! — he *was*, in spite of everything, a good and noble man.

KURT: In spite of everything? He was brave too. The way he fought, for himself, and for others.

ALICE: What miseries he suffered! And what humiliations! And he blotted them out — so that he could go on living.

KURT: He was a man whom life passed by. That explains much, Alice. Go in to him.

ALICE: No. I can't. Because while we've been speaking here, I suddenly remembered him as he was when he was young. I've been seeing him, I see him now, as he was when he was twenty. I must have loved that man.

KURT: And hated him.

ALICE: And hated him. Peace be with him.

She walks towards the door right, and stops there, with clasped hands.

A Dream Play

(1901)

Introduction to
A DREAM PLAY

S TRINDBERG wrote A DREAM PLAY in 1901, at the
age of fifty-two. It was his favourite among all his
works; in a letter to his publisher, Karl-Otto Bonnier,
on 31 August 1906, he said that he prized it more than anything he had written, and on 17 April 1907 he described it
to his German translator, Emil Schering, as "my most
beloved play, child of my greatest pain". The matter and
mood of it stemmed directly from his third, final and vol-
canic marriage, with the Norwegian actress Harriet Bosse.

In 1900, while searching for someone to act the Lady
in TO DAMASCUS, which was shortly to be staged by
the Dramatic Theatre, he had seen Harriet, then aged twenty-
two*, act Puck in A MIDSUMMER NIGHT'S DREAM. He
at once chose her for the Lady; the same year, he wrote
EASTER for her; and the following May they married. But
the marriage was a failure, as his two earlier ones had been;
he was nearly thirty years older than Harriet, and she was
as domineering a personality as he was. "We are now con-
vinced that our union will be a lasting one, for we are living
in complete harmony," he wrote in his diary on 25 June;
but the following day she left him "without saying goodbye,
without saying where she was going"; returned to him in
August, pregnant, but left again the same month. "I
cannot be trampled in the dirt," she wrote to him on 27
August. "Rather than face a horrible future, full of unjust
insults and pain for us both, I am going now, while I still
have fresh in my memory all you have given me that is
beautiful." Ten days later Strindberg bitterly noted in his
diary:

"E. V. Hartman says that love is a farce invented by
nature to fool men and women into propagating their

*She is sometimes described as having been nineteen when they met,
but she was born on 19 February 1878.

species. Life disgusts me and has always done so. Everything is worthless ! . . . People are not born wicked, but
life makes them wicked. So life cannot be an education,
nor can it be a punishment (which improves); it is simply
an evil! . . . Resignation! Yes, that is what I tried last. But
if you put up with everything, you have in the end to
endure filth and humiliation, and that is what you have
no right to do!"

He meditated suicide much that autumn. "The impulse
to die by my own hand grows stronger," he noted on 25
September. "It will soon be irresistible . . . My blood shall
atone for my past, and with my blood my longing for evil
will be obliterated . . . I have lived as I could, and not as I
should have wished." Yet on 4 October he dined with
Harriet and they made love; and the following day, three
and a half months' pregnant, she returned to live with him.
Such was the background against which, over the next six
and a half weeks, he composed A DREAM PLAY.

He based it on a straightforward realistic play which
he had drafted earlier in the year, entitled THE CORRIDOR
DRAMA. In this, a composer has been waiting seven years
for his opera to be performed, and seven years for a wife.
Now his opera has been accepted, he has become engaged,
and is waiting at the theatre for his fiancée, a singer who
has achieved success in his opera; as a sequel to their mutual
triumph, they are to marry and go to the south. But she
does not come; the summer passes, the roses wither, and at
last he hears that she has gone abroad alone. The composer
dies, and the stage-door keeper scatters roses over him.
Strindberg stopped work on this when Harriet first left
him that June, took it up again, according to his diary, on
22 August a few hours before he received a letter from
Harriet telling him that she had left him for good, and
finally, after their reunion in October, re-worked it as
A DREAM PLAY (though when he completed it on 18
November he called it THE RISING CASTLE).

In a short preface to the play, he explained his
intention:

"In this dream play, the author has, as in his former

dream play, TO DAMASCUS, attempted to imitate the inconsequent yet transparently logical shape of a dream. Everything can happen, everything is possible and probable. Time and place do not exist; on an insignificant basis of reality, the imagination spins, weaving new patterns; a mixture of memories, experiences, free fancies, incongruities and improvisations. The characters split, double, multiply, evaporate, condense, disperse, assemble. But one consciousness rules over them all, that of the dreamer; for him there are no secrets, no illogicalities, no scruples, no laws. He neither acquits nor condemns, but merely relates; and, as a dream is more often painful than happy, so an undertone of melancholy and of pity for all mortal beings accompanies this flickering tale."

Strindberg had long been preoccupied with dreams, He had studied with fascination Edgar Allan Poe's treatment of them (Poe was, with Dickens, one of his favourite authors) and, in 1899 he had been greatly impressed by Rudyard Kipling's story THE BRUSHWOOD BOY, in which two people have the same dream in which they meet. This pre-occupation had been intensified since his meeting with Harriet; he had felt that he was moving in a dream world. A week after their engagement, on 13 March 1901, he wrote: "In what land of dreams I am living I know not, but I dread descending again to reality." And on 2 November 1901, a fortnight before he finished A DREAM PLAY, he wrote to the painter Carl Larsson: "Life becomes more and more dreamlike and inexplicable to me. Perhaps death really is the awakening." His diary during this year is full of details of his own dreams; and on 18 November, the day he finished A DREAM PLAY he noted:

Am reading about Indian religions.

The whole world is but a semblance (= Humbug or relative emptiness). The primary Divine Power (Maham-Atma, Tad, Aum, Brama), allowed itself to be seduced by Maya, or the impulse of procreation.

Thus the Divine Primary Element sinned against

itself. (Love is sin, therefore the pangs of love are the greatest of all hells.)

The world has come into existence only through Sin — if in fact it exists at all — for it is really only a dream picture (consequently my DREAM PLAY is a picture of life), a phantom, and the ascetic's allotted task is to destroy it. But this task conflicts with the love impulse, and the sum total of it all is a ceaseless wavering between sensual orgies and the anguish of repentance.

This would seem to be the riddle of the world.

I turned up the above in [Arvid Ahnfelt's] History of Literature, just as I was about to finish my Dream Play, THE GROWING CASTLE, on the morning of the 18th. On this same morning I saw the Castle (= Horseguards' Barracks) illuminated, as it were, by the rising sun.

Indian religion, therefore, showed me the meaning of my DREAM PLAY, and the significance of Indra's Daughter, and the Secret of the Door = Nothingness.

Read Buddhism all day.

The dream technique, with its swift and apparently irrelevant cutting from one scene to another, was, as Strindberg stated in his preface to A DREAM PLAY, something that he had practised in TO DAMASCUS, where likewise we can never be sure what is real and what is imagined. For years he had been fascinated by magic lanterns, with their similar capacity to provide seemingly disconnected yet suggestively relevant images. On 14 September 1904 he referred to them to describe his own idyllic memories of that summer. "Those were only magic lantern pictures I gave you from Furusund. *Förvandlingsbilder,* dissolving views.* But that's what life is."

As with every play that Strindberg wrote (including

*Thus in the Swedish original; Strindberg added the English words "dissolving views" as a translation of *förvandlingsbilder,* which literally means "transformation pictures".

some twenty historical ones), A DREAM PLAY includes
much that is identifiable as direct personal experience. The
"Rising Castle" in which the Officer is imprisoned was, as
his diary implies, the new cavalry barracks with its gilded
onion-shaped dome ("the most beautiful building in
Stockholm", he called it in an essay), which he could see
from his windows in Karlavägen. Like the Officer, he had
waited in the corridor of the Royal Theatre, first for Siri
more than twenty years before, and more recently for
Harriet. There was a door there with a clover-shaped
hole, and he had often wondered where it led to.
Fairhaven, to which the Officer flees with Agnes, was
the coastal resort of Fagervik (literally "Fair Bay"), just
outside Stockholm. Strindberg used to stay there with his
brother-in-law, Hugo Philp, who on gaining his doctorate
in 1896 had become a schoolmaster and had had to re-
learn his early and forgotten knowledge in order to teach
beginners. Strindberg himself had a recurrent nightmare of
finding himself a schoolboy again, threatened by the cane;
hence the classroom scene, where the Officer sits at a small
desk, unable to multiply two by two. At Fagervik he
had met a jeweller and art collector named Christian Hammer,
who owned the island, and had lost his sight. He too was
to appear in the play, as the Blind Man. In 1899, Strindberg
had seen the Baths Doctor there, Elias Nordström, go to a
ball wearing a Moorish mask; hence the Quarantine Master,
Ordström, with his blackened face and sulphur ovens
(there had been a cholera outbreak at Fagervik some years
before). Opposite Fagervik lay Skarmsund, which Strindberg, by the removal of a single letter, altered to Skamsund
(literally Shame-Sound = Foulstrand). The incident of the
degree ceremony probably stemmed from a rumour which
had reached Strindberg's ears the previous year that he was
to be given a doctorate at the University of Lund. The
childhood scene with the Officer's parents is directly autobiographical; so are the marriage scenes between the
Advocate and Agnes. Strindberg once stated that a carefree
lieutenant named Jean Lundin, whom he had known
twenty years earlier when he was writing THE RED ROOM,

was the original of the Officer; but Strindberg himself
was the principal original of that character, and of the
Advocate and the Poet (as of most of his leading male
characters, in everything he wrote).

Like PEER GYNT, the last act of which is also a
dream play, Strindberg's A DREAM PLAY was regarded,
on publication, as unstageable, and it was not until more
than five years later, on 17 April 1907, that it received its
first performance, with Harriet Bosse in the dual role of
Indra's Daughter and Agnes. Strindberg, following his
usual custom, did not attend (he seldom saw any of his
plays after the dress rehearsal); but he noted in his diary:
"At 11 o'clock this evening Harriet, Castengren [the
director] and Ranft [the theatre owner] telephoned to
say that A DREAM PLAY had been a success. T.b.t.g.
[Thanks be to God] !" There had been problems; Castengren
had planned to use magic lantern slides to provide the
various scenic effects, but the German apparatus gave
trouble in rehearsal, and they had to resort to ordinary
décor which, Strindberg recorded in his OPEN LETTERS
TO THE INTIMATE THEATRE, "disturbed the actors'
mood and caused interminable intervals; moreover, the
whole thing became materialized, instead of the intended
opposite, i.e. dematerialization". Yet the audience admired
it, and at first refused to leave until the author had taken
his call, so that Albert Ranft had to come forward and
promise to telephone their approbation to him.

In 1921 Max Reinhardt, whose productions of THE
DANCE OF DEATH, THE PELICAN and THE GHOST
SONATA had established him as a Strindberg pioneer,
directed A DREAM PLAY in Stockholm; but it had a
mixed reception, and the first really successful performance was in 1935 when Olof Molander, a great Strindberg director, staged it in the Swedish capital, underlin-
ing the realism of the play by using immediately
recognizable Stockholm locations against a background of
darkness pierced only by the occasional spotlight, with an
imaginative use of the forestage so that the characters
sometimes seemed to move out of their surroundings into

the audience. Molander directed four further productions
of the play during the next twenty years, in each instance
using the full technical resources of the theatre, so that
A DREAM PLAY came to be thought of as a "spectacular".
I saw Molander's final production, in 1955, and remember
its huge and varied visual effects. It was a very impressive,
very long evening; one watched the spectacle with
admiration but no sense of involvement; the play seemed
remote and dated. Nor was the effect different when
Ingmar Bergman directed it for Swedish television in 1963,
with Ingrid Thulin as Indra's Daughter and Agnes — a
production which the director himself regarded as a failure.

In 1970 Bergman directed the play again, on stage at
the Royal Theatre of Stockholm, and this time he treated
it very differently. He presented it in the small studio
auditorium of the Royal Theatre, which seats only three
hundred and fifty people, judiciously cut and without an
interval, so that the performance lasted under two hours,
and virtually without décor. In other words, laying his
usual emphasis on close personal contact between actors
and audience, he offered it not as a spectacular but as a
chamber play like THE GHOST SONATA, and the
difference was extraordinary. What had previously seemed
verbose and antiquated now sprang to life. For décor, he
used only a black backdrop with the minimum of
properties, varied by a white backdrop for the scenes at
Fairhaven, the inhabitants of which were likewise dressed
in white. He dispensed totally with Strindberg's elaborate
stage directions, such as "the flower bud on the roof
blossoms forth into a huge chrysanthemum", which made
the play seem particularly old-fashioned when I saw the
Molander production in 1955, and considerably shortened
the final third of the play. Bergman's adaptation has been
published in English (Secker & Warburg, London, The
Dial Press, New York and P. A. Norstedt, Stockholm,
1973), and to my mind works far better on the stage than
the full version as printed here; some great plays (BRAND
is another) need bold cutting and transposition for their
stageability (as opposed to their literary worth) to become

apparent, and students may find it instructive to compare
that imaginative and poetically faithful adaptation with
Strindberg's full original — remembering Strindberg's
advice to August Falck when the latter was about to direct
the first Swedish production of THE FATHER in 1887:
"Cut more if you wish! You'll hear at rehearsal what doesn't
work."

A DREAM PLAY had a humble London premiere, when
Pax Robertson bravely presented it at her Chelsea Arts
Theatre in 1930, and G. R. Schjelderup directed a single per-
formance at the Grafton Theatre (off the Tottenham Court
Road) in 1933, with Donald Wolfit as the Officer. It was
performed on English sound radio in 1948, 1957 and 1982.
Ingmar Bergman's Swedish production visited the Aldwych
Theatre during the World Theatre Season of 1971, and
created a memorable impression, and on 2 May 1974 Michael
Ockrent directed it excitingly at the Traverse Theatre, Edinburgh, using only nine players to portray the more-than-
forty characters — a production that was successfully revived
later in the year for the Edinburgh Festival. Ockrent
employed the unusual device of having three actresses play
Agnes simultaneously on three different physical levels and
in different characterizations, to suggest her various aspects.
Cordelia Oliver in the *Guardian* described the performance
as "gripping the imagination from the first moment when,
one by one, on different levels like hallucinations, the
intense faces of the women float, disembodied, in the black-
ness", and Irving Wardle in the *Times* praised its "violently
abrupt changes of rhythm, particularly where it erupts into
Parisian gallops and blazing organ sonorities", and its
"startling expressionistic imagery". Completely different in
conception from the Bergman production, it did not suffer
by comparison. London did not see a full-scale production
until 1985, when John Barton staged the play strangely
disappointingly for the Royal Shakespeare Company at the
Barbican Pit.

AUTHOR'S NOTE

In this dream play the author has, as in his former
dream play, TO DAMASCUS, attempted to imitate the
inconsequent yet transparently logical shape of a dream.
Everything can happen, everything is possible and probable.
Time and place do not exist; on an insignificant basis of
reality the imagination spins, weaving new patterns; a mixture of memories, experiences, free fancies, incongruities
and improvisations. The characters split, double, multiply,
evaporate, condense, disperse, assemble. But one consciousness rules over them all, that of the dreamer; for him
there are no secrets, no illogicalities, no scruples, no laws.
He neither acquits nor condemns, but merely relates; and,
just as a dream is more often painful than happy, so an
undertone of melancholy and of pity for all mortal beings
accompanies this flickering tale. Sleep, the liberator,
often seems a tormentor, but when the agony is harshest
comes the awakening and reconciles the sufferer with
reality — which, however painful, is yet a mercy, compared
with the agony of the dream.

A Dream Play

(1901)

This translation of A DREAM PLAY was first
performed, in an adaptation by Ingmar Bergman, at the
Lyric Players Theatre, Belfast, on 28 February 1973. The
cast was:

THE POET	Hamish Roughead
AGNES	Kathleen McClay
GLAZIER	Michael Duffy
OFFICER	Pitt Wilkinson
FATHER	Louis Rolston
MOTHER	Trudy Kelly
LINA	Maureen Dow
INDRA	Peter Templar
INDRA'S DAUGHTER	Linda Wray
STAGE-DOOR KEEPER	Maureen Dow
BILL-POSTER	Peter Templar
VICTORIA	Pat Smylie
DANCER	Pat Smylie
SINGER	Trudy Kelly
PROMPTER	Clem Davies
POLICEMAN	William Walker
ADVOCATE	John Franklyn
KRISTIN	Trudy Kelly
QUARANTINE MASTER	John Keenan
FIRST SICK MAN	Alan Bryce
SECOND SICK MAN	Peter Templar
DON JUAN	Maurice O'Callaghan
COQUETTE	Maureen Dow
HE	Clem Davies
PENSIONER	Michael Duffy
FIRST COAL-CARRIER	William Hamilton
SECOND COAL-CARRIER	William Walker
GENTLEMAN	Alan Bryce
HIS WIFE	Maureen Dow
EDITH	Pat Smylie
HER MOTHER	Trudy Kelly
NAVAL OFFICER	John Pine

ALICE	Alison Kelly
BLIND MAN	Louis Rolston
SCHOOLMASTER	Maurice O'Callaghan
BOYS	Andrew Kennedy, John O'Reilly, John O'Rourke
CHANCELLOR	Alex McClay
DEAN OF THEOLOGY	Pat Brannigan
DEAN OF PHILOSOPHY	William Hamilton
DEAN OF MEDICINE	Maurice O'Callaghan
DEAN OF LAW	John Pine

Designed by John L. Stark
Directed by Donald Bodley

On 2 May 1974 it was performed at the Traverse Theatre, Edinburgh. The cast was:

POET	Roger Kemp
AGNES	Maggie Jordan Janet Amsden Susan Carpenter
GLAZIER QUARANTINE MASTER SCHOOLMASTER A COAL-CARRIER	Simon Callow
OFFICER	James Snell
FATHER ADVOCATE A GENTLEMAN	Roy Marsden
BILL-POSTER A COAL-CARRIER BLIND MAN	Richard Vanstone
LINA KRISTIN EDITH	Lyndy Lawson

Designed by Poppy Mitchell
Directed by Michael Ockrent

CHARACTERS

INDRA
*INDRA'S DAUGHTER
*AGNES
THE GLAZIER
THE OFFICER
HIS FATHER
HIS MOTHER
LINA
THE STAGE-DOOR KEEPER
THE BILL-POSTER
A BALLET DANCER
A SINGER
A PROMPTER
A POLICEMAN
THE ADVOCATE
KRISTIN
THE QUARANTINE MASTER
A DANDY
A COQUETTE
HER "FRIEND"
THE POET
HE
SHE
A PENSIONER
EDITH
EDITH'S MOTHER
A NAVAL OFFICER
ALICE
THE SCHOOLMASTER
A NEWLY-MARRIED HUSBAND
A NEWLY-MARRIED WIFE
THE BLIND MAN

*The parts of Indra's Daughter and Agnes are sometimes doubled, sometimes played by separate actresses. (Translator's note)

FIRST COAL-CARRIER
SECOND COAL-CARRIER
A GENTLEMAN
HIS WIFE
THE CHANCELLOR
DEAN OF THEOLOGY
DEAN OF PHILOSOPHY
DEAN OF MEDICINE
DEAN OF LAW

DANCERS, SINGERS, CLERKS, CHILDREN,
SCHOOLBOYS, SAILORS, ETC.

PRELUDE

[*A background of banks of cloud like crumbling slate mountains, with ruined castles and fortresses. The constellations of Leo, Virgo and Libra are visible. Between them shining brightly, is the planet Jupiter.* INDRA'S DAUGHTER *is standing on the topmost cloud.*] *

INDRA'S VOICE [*from above*]:
Where are you, daughter, where?

INDRA'S DAUGHTER:
Here, Father, here!

INDRA'S VOICE:
You have lost your way, child. Take care, you are falling.
How did you come here?

INDRA'S DAUGHTER:
I followed the lightning flash from furthest space,
And rode upon a cloud.
But the cloud began to fall, and I fall with it.
Say, mighty father, Indra, what strange regions
Are these? The air is sparse and hard to breathe.

INDRA'S VOICE:
You have left the second world and entered the third.
Beyond Cukra, the morning star,
You have passed far, and enter now
The vaporous realm of earth. [Mark there
The seventh house of the sun, that men call Libra.
The day-star stands at the balance-point of autumn,
When day and night weigh equal.]

*The passages enclosed in bold brackets, [ ], are those cut by Ingmar Bergman in his adaptation of the play (see introduction). He also made numerous transpositions which it has been impracticable to indicate here.

INDRA'S DAUGHTER:
>   You said the earth. Is that this dark
>   And gloomy world illumined by the moon?

INDRA'S VOICE:
>   It is the densest and the heaviest
>   Of the spheres that roam in space.

[INDRA'S DAUGHTER:
>   Does the sun never shine there?

INDRA'S VOICE:
>   The sun shines there indeed, but not perpetually.

INDRA'S DAUGHTER:
>   The cloud is parting, and I see down there —

INDRA'S VOICE:
>   What do you see, child?

INDRA'S DAUGHTER:
>   I see ... that there is beauty. Green forests,
>   Blue waters, white mountains and yellow fields —

INDRA'S VOICE:
>   Yes. It is fair, like all that Brahma made.
>   But it was once yet fairer there,
>   In the morn of time. Then something happened.
>   A shaking of the orbit; perhaps more.
>   Revolt followed by crime, that had to be quelled.]

INDRA'S DAUGHTER:
>   Now I hear sounds from down there.
>   What race dwells there?

INDRA'S VOICE:
>   Descend and see.
>   I speak no ill of the Creator's children.
>   But what you hear rise upwards is their speech.

INDRA'S DAUGHTER:
>   It sounds like ... It has not a joyful sound.

[INDRA'S VOICE:
>   You do not surprise me. Their mother tongue

Is named complaint. The people of the earth
Are a discontented and ungrateful race.

INDRA'S DAUGHTER:

Do not say so. Now I hear cries of joy,
And shots, and boomings. I see lightnings flash.
Bells ring, and fires are lit, and many thousand
Thousand voices sing praise and thanks to heaven.
[Pause.]
You judge them harshly, Father.]

INDRA'S VOICE:

Descend and see, and hear, and then return,
And tell me, child, if their complaints
And wailings are well-founded.

[INDRA'S DAUGHTER:

I shall obey and go. But come with me, Father.

INDRA'S VOICE:

No, I cannot breathe there.]

INDRA'S DAUGHTER:

The cloud is falling, the air grows close, I choke.
I breathe no air, but only smoke and water,
So heavy, that it drags me down, and down,
And now I can discern its heeling mass.
Ah, this third world is not the best —

INDRA'S VOICE:

It is not the best, for sure, but not the worst.
[It is called dust, it wheels like all the rest,
And so its people are sometimes seized with dizziness,
And hover between imbalance and madness.]
Have courage, child. It is but a trial.

INDRA'S DAUGHTER [on her knees, as the cloud sinks]:
I'm falling!

[The backcloth now shows a forest of gigantic holly-
hocks in bloom — white, pink, purple, sulphur-yellow,

*violet. Above them can be seen the gilded roof of a
castle, topped by a flower-bud shaped like a crown.
Beneath the walls of the castle piles of straw are
spread, covering the manure removed from the stables.
The wings, which remain the same throughout the
play, are stylized wall-paintings which simultaneously
represent interiors, exteriors and landscape.]*

The GLAZIER *and* INDRA'S DAUGHTER *enter.*

DAUGHTER: The castle is still rising from the earth.
Father, do you see how much it has grown since last
year?

GLAZIER [*to himself*] : I've never seen that castle before
. . . never heard of a castle rising . . . but — [*to the*
DAUGHTER *with conviction.*] Yes, it has grown eight
feet, but that's because they've manured it. And if you
look carefully, you'll see that a wing has grown on the
side facing the sun.

DAUGHTER: Won't it flower soon? We're past midsummer.

GLAZIER: Don't you see the flower up there?

DAUGHTER: Yes, I see it! [*Claps her hands.*] Father, why
do flowers grow out of dirt?

GLAZIER [*piously*] : Because they don't like the dirt, so
they run up into the light as fast as they can, to blossom
and die.

DAUGHTER: Do you know who lives in the castle?

GLAZIER: I did once, but I've forgotten.

DAUGHTER: I think there's a prisoner inside. I'm sure
he's waiting for me to free him.

GLAZIER: But at what price?

DAUGHTER: One doesn't bargain about one's duty. Let's
go into the castle.

GLAZIER: Yes, let's go.

They go towards the rear of the stage, which gradually opens out towards the wings, revealing a simple, bare room with a table and a few chairs. On one of the chairs sits an OFFICER *in a highly unusual modern uniform. He is rocking in his chair and striking the table with his sabre.*

DAUGHTER [*goes to the* OFFICER *and gently takes the sabre from his hand*]: You mustn't, you mustn't.

OFFICER: Please, Agnes, let me keep my sword.

DAUGHTER: No, you'll break the table. [*To her* FATHER.] Go down to the harness-room and put the window in, and we'll meet later. [*The* GLAZIER *goes.*] You are a prisoner in your room. I have come to free you.

OFFICER: I suppose I've been waiting for that. But I wasn't sure you'd want to.

DAUGHTER: The castle is strong, it has seven walls, but — we'll manage. Do you want to or not?

OFFICER: To be honest, I don't know. Either way I'll suffer. Every joy in life must be paid for with a double portion of sorrow. Sitting here is hard, but if I buy my freedom I'll have to suffer threefold. Agnes, I'd rather stay here, if only I can see you.

DAUGHTER: What do you see in me?

OFFICER: [The beauty which is the harmony of the universe. There are lines in your figure which I find only in the orbits of the solar system, in the sound of a violin, in the vibrations of light.] You are a child of God —

DAUGHTER: So are you.

OFFICER: Then why must I guard horses? Clean stables, and shovel manure?

DAUGHTER: So that you shall long to get away.

OFFICER: I do long, but it's so hard to break the habit.

DAUGHTER: But it's a duty to seek freedom in the light.

OFFICER: Duty? Life has never shown any sense of duty towards me.

DAUGHTER: You feel life has been unjust to you?

OFFICER: Yes! It has been unjust.

[*Voices are now heard behind the screen dividing off the rest of the stage. It is drawn aside, and the* OFFICER *and the* DAUGHTER *look at what it reveals and stand frozen, their expressions also frozen.*

At a table sits the MOTHER, *ill. Before her burns a tallow candle, which she now and then trims with a pair of candle-scissors. On the table lie piles of newly-sewn shirts, which she is marking with marking-ink and a goose quill. Left stands a brown clothes-cupboard.*]

FATHER [*offers her a silk cloak, gently*]: You don't want it?

MOTHER: A silk cloak for me, my dear? What's the use? I shall die soon.

FATHER: You believe what the doctor says?

MOTHER [*touches her breast*]: I believe the voice that speaks in here.

FATHER [*sadly*]: And you think of your children, first and always.

MOTHER: They've been my life, my justification, my joy and my grief.

FATHER: Kristina, forgive me — for everything.

MOTHER: Oh, my dear. Forgive me, dearest. We have tormented each other. Why? We don't know. We couldn't do otherwise. But here are the children's new clothes. See they change twice a week, on Wednesday and

Sunday, and that Louisa washes them — all over. Are you going out?

FATHER: I must go up to the college. It's eleven o'clock.

MOTHER: Ask Alfred to come in before you go.

FATHER [*points at the* OFFICER]: Here he is, the little dear.

MOTHER: My eyes are starting to go, too. Yes, it's getting dark. [*Trims the candle.*] Alfred. Come here.

The FATHER *goes out through the middle of the wall, nodding goodbye. The* OFFICER *goes over to the* MOTHER.

MOTHER: Who is that girl?

OFFICER [*whispers*]: It is Agnes.

MOTHER: Oh, is it Agnes? Do you know what they say? That she's the God Indra's daughter, who asked to be allowed to come down to earth to see what human life is really like. But don't say anything.

OFFICER: She is a god's child!

MOTHER [*aloud*]: Alfred dear, I shall soon be leaving you and your brothers and sisters. Let me give you some advice.

OFFICER [*sadly*]: Yes, Mother.

[MOTHER: It's just this. Never strive with God.

OFFICER: What do you mean, Mother?]

MOTHER: You mustn't go round feeling life has been unjust to you.

OFFICER: But when people do treat me unjustly?

MOTHER: You're thinking of the time you were unjustly punished for stealing a penny that was later found?

OFFICER: Yes. And that injustice warped my whole life.

MOTHER: I know. But now go to that cupboard —

OFFICER [*embarrassed*] : You know, then? It's —

MOTHER: *The Swiss Family Robinson*. Which —

OFFICER: Don't go on.

MOTHER: Which your brother got punished for — and which you'd torn up and hidden.

OFFICER: Fancy that cupboard still standing there after twenty years. We've moved so often, and my mother died ten years ago.

MOTHER: Well, what of it? You always have to ask questions about everything. That way you'll ruin the best life has to offer. Ah, here's Lina.

LINA [*enters*] : Please, madam. It's very kind of you, but I can't go to the christening —

MOTHER: Why not, child?

LINA: I've nothing to wear.

MOTHER: You can borrow this cloak of mine.

LINA: Oh, madam, I can't do that.

MOTHER: I don't understand. I shall never go to any more parties —

OFFICER: What will Father say? It's a gift from him —

[MOTHER: He wouldn't be so small -minded.]

FATHER [*puts his head in*] : Are you lending my gift to the servant?

MOTHER: Don't speak like that. Remember I was once a servant too. Why must you hurt someone who is innocent?

FATHER: Why must you hurt me, your husband?

MOTHER: Oh, this life! When one does a good deed, there's always someone for whom it's ugly. Help one person, you hurt another. Ah, this life!

[*She trims the candle so that it goes out. The stage is darkened and the screen is drawn again.*]

DAUGHTER: Alas for mankind!

OFFICER: You think so?

DAUGHTER: Yes. Life is hard — but love conquers all! Come and see.

[*The backcloth is raised, revealing a shabby wall. In the middle of it is a gate opening onto a green area bathed in light, and containing an enormous blue monk's-hood or aconite. To the left of the gate sits a female* STAGE-DOOR KEEPER, *with a shawl over head and shoulders, knitting another and more elaborate shawl. On the right is a cylindrical bill-hoarding, which the* BILL-POSTER *is cleaning. Beside him stands a fishing-net with a green handle. Further to the right is a door with air-holes in the form of a four-leaved clover. Left of the gate stands a slender lime-tree with a pitch-black trunk and a few light-green leaves. Next to it is a manhole.*]

DAUGHTER [*walks over to the* STAGE-DOOR KEEPER]: Isn't that shawl ready yet?

STAGE-DOOR KEEPER: Why, no, my dear. Twenty-six years is no time for such a task.

DAUGHTER: And your lover never came back?

STAGE-DOOR KEEPER: No, but it wasn't his fault. He *had* to go away, poor man. That was thirty years ago.

DAUGHTER [*to the* BILL-POSTER]: Wasn't she a dancer? Up there, in the opera?

BILL-POSTER: She was the star. But when he went, he seemed to take her dancing with him. And she never got any more parts.

DAUGHTER: Everyone complains. With their eyes, if not their tongues.

BILL-POSTER: I don't complain. Not now, since I got a fish-chest and a green fishing-net.

DAUGHTER: And that makes you happy?

BILL-POSTER: Oh, yes, so happy! It was the dream of my youth. And now it's come true. Of course, I'm — fifty now—

DAUGHTER: Fifty years for a fish-chest and a fishing net —

BILL-POSTER: A green fishing-net, a green one.

DAUGHTER [to the STAGE-DOOR KEEPER]: Give me the shawl, then I can sit here and watch the people. But you must stand behind and tell me about them. [Takes the shawl and seats herself beside the gate.]

STAGE-DOOR KEEPER: Today's the last day before the theatre closes. Now they learn whether they're being kept on or not —

DAUGHTER: What happens to those who aren't?

STAGE-DOOR KEEPER: Blessed Jesus, you'll see. [I'll put the shawl over your head.]

DAUGHTER: Poor people.

STAGE-DOOR KEEPER: Look, here comes one. She's not one of the chosen. See how she's crying.

The SINGER *runs in from the right and out through the door with her handkerchief to her eyes. She stops a moment in the passage outside the door and leans her head against the wall, then hurries out.*

DAUGHTER: Alas for mankind!

STAGE-DOOR KEEPER: But look at this one. There's a happy man.

The OFFICER *enters through the door, in frock-coat and top-hat, carrying a bouquet of roses, radiant and happy.*

STAGE-DOOR KEEPER: He is to marry Miss Victoria.

OFFICER [*downstage, looks up and sings*] : Victoria!

STAGE-DOOR KEEPER: She'll be right down.

OFFICER: Good, good. The carriage is waiting, the table laid, the champagne on ice. May I embrace you, ladies? [*Embraces the* DAUGHTER *and the* STAGE-DOOR KEEPER. *Sings.*] Victoria!

A GIRL'S VOICE [*from above, sings*]: I am here!

OFFICER [*begins to stroll around*]: Ah, well. I'll wait.

DAUGHTER: Do you know me?

OFFICER: No, I know only one woman. Victoria! For seven years I have walked here and waited for her — at noon, when the sun stood above the chimneys, and at evening, when the gloom of night began to fall. Look at the floor here, you can see the footprints of the faithful lover. Hurrah! She is mine! [*Sings.*] Victoria! [*He gets no reply.*] Well, she's getting dressed. [*To the* BILL-POSTER.] You've a fishing-net, I see. Everyone at the opera house is crazy about fishing-nets — or rather fish! They like dumb fish, because they can't sing. What does a thing like that cost?

BILL-POSTER: It's quite expensive.

OFFICER [*sings*]: Victoria! [[*Shakes the lime-tree.*] Look — it's coming into leaf again. For the eighth time.] Victoria! Now she's combing her fringe. [*To the* DAUGHTER.] Come, madam, let me go up and fetch my bride.

STAGE-DOOR KEEPER: No one's allowed on to the stage.

OFFICER: Seven years I have been walking here. Seven times three hundred and sixty-five makes two thousand five hundred and fifty-five! [*Stops and points at the door with the clover-shaped holes.*] And that door I've stared at two thousand five hundred and fifty-five times, without discovering where it leads to. And that clover-leaf to let in light. For whom does it let in light? Is there some-one inside? Does someone live there?

STAGE-DOOR KEEPER: I don't know. I've never seen it opened.

OFFICER: It looks like a pantry door I saw when I was four and went away one Sunday afternoon with the maid. Away, to [other families and] other maids, but I never got beyond the kitchens, and I sat between the water-cask and the salt-barrel. I've seen so many kitchens in my time, and the pantries were always in the porch, with bored round holes and a clover-leaf. But the opera house has no pantry, for they have no kitchen. [*Sings.*] Victoria! Tell me, she can't go out any other way but this, can she?

STAGE-DOOR KEEPER: No there's no other way.

OFFICER: Good, then I shan't miss her. [DANCERS, *etc.*, *hurry out and are quizzed by the* OFFICER.] Now she must be here soon. I say! That flower out there, that blue monk's-hood. I haven't seen that since I was a child. Is it the same one? I remember in a parsonage, when I was seven — two doves, on it, blue doves under that hood — but once a bee came and crept into the hood. Then I thought, "Now I have you!", so I pinched the flower shut; but the bee stung through it and I cried. But then the parson's wife came and put wet earth on it — and we had wild strawberries and milk for supper. I think it's getting dark already. [*To the* BILL-POSTER.] Where are you going?

BILL-POSTER: Home for supper.

OFFICER [*feels his eyes*]: Supper? At this time of day? Look — may I go in for a moment and telephone to the rising castle?

DAUGHTER: What do you want there?

OFFICER: I must tell the glazier to put in double windows, for it'll soon be winter and I'm so terribly cold. [*Goes to the* STAGE-DOOR KEEPER'S *lodge.*]

DAUGHTER: Who is Miss Victoria?

STAGE-DOOR KEEPER: The girl he loves.

DAUGHTER: Well answered. What she may be to us and others, he doesn't care. All she is, is what she is to him.

[*It grows rapidly dark.*]

STAGE-DOOR KEEPER [*lights lamp*]: It's getting dark quickly today.

[DAUGHTER: To the gods a year is as a minute.

STAGE-DOOR KEEPER: And to humans a minute can be as a year.]

The OFFICER *returns. He looks dusty, the roses are withered.*

OFFICER: She hasn't come yet?

STAGE-DOOR KEEPER: No.

OFFICER: She'll *come. She'll* come. [*Wanders about.*] But perhaps I'd better cancel the lunch. As it's already evening. Yes, I'll do that. [*Goes in and telephones.*]

STAGE-DOOR KEEPER [*to the* DAUGHTER]: May I have my shawl now?

DAUGHTER: No, [take a little time off,] I'll do your job. I want to learn to know people and life, to find out if it's as hard as they say.

STAGE-DOOR KEEPER: But you mustn't sleep at your post here. Never sleep, night or day —

DAUGHTER: Not sleep at night?

STAGE-DOOR KEEPER: Yes, if you can, with the bell-rope round your wrist — there are night-watchmen on the stage and they're relieved every three hours.

DAUGHTER: But that's inhuman —

STAGE-DOOR KEEPER: You may think so, but folk like

me are glad of such a job, and if you knew how envied I
am —

DAUGHTER: Envied? [For doing this?]

STAGE-DOOR KEEPER: Yes. But, you know, what's
worse than the hours and the drudgery and the draughts
and the cold and the damp is being everybody's
confidante. They come to me — why? [Perhaps they
read in the lines of my face the runes of suffering that
invite confidences.] That shawl hides thirty years of
sorrows, mine and others'.

DAUGHTER: It's heavy too, and it burns like nettles.

STAGE-DOOR KEEPER: Wear it if you wish. When it
gets too heavy, give me a shout and I'll come and relieve
you.

DAUGHTER: [Goodbye.] What you can bear, I surely
can.

STAGE-DOOR KEEPER: We'll see. But be kind to my
little friends, and don't yawn at their sorrows.

*She disappears down the passage. [The stage is
darkened and the scene changes so that the lime-tree
is bare of leaves and the monk's-hood almost withered.
When the lights go up, the foliage outside is autumn-
brown.] The* OFFICER *enters. Now he has grey hair
and a grey beard. His clothes are dilapidated, his shirt-
collar black and limp, the bouquet of roses so withered
that only the branches remain. He wanders around.*

OFFICER: From all the evidence, summer is past and
autumn near. [I see that from that lime-tree and that
monk's-hood.] [*Wanders.*] But the autumn is my spring.
Then the theatre will open again! And then she must
come. Kind lady, may I sit on this chair for a little while?

DAUGHTER: Sit, my friend. I can stand.

OFFICER [*sits*] : If only I could sleep a little, things would be better. [*Sleeps for a second, then jumps up and starts wandering again. Stops before the door with the clover-leaf and points.*] This door, that gives me no peace. What is behind it? There must be something. [*Soft music is heard from above, in dance rhythm.*] Ah! Now the rehearsals have begun. [[*The stage is spasmodically illuminated as by a lighthouse.*] What is this? [*Follows the changing light.*] Light and darkness — light and darkness?

DAUGHTER [*similarly*] : Day and night. Day and night. A merciful Providence wishes to shorten your waiting; so the days flee the pursuing nights.

> *The stage remains illuminated.*] *The* BILL-POSTER *enters with his fishing-net and bill-posting equipment.*

OFFICER: There's the bill-poster with his fishing-net. Had good fishing?

BILL-POSTER: Oh, yes. The summer was hot and a little long. The net was very good, but not quite as I'd imagined —

OFFICER [*stresses the words*] : Not quite as I'd imagined. Excellently said. Nothing is as I had imagined. Because the thought is more than the deed — bigger than the fact. [*Wanders round and slaps the bouquet against the walls so that the last leaves fall.*]

BILL-POSTER: Hasn't she come down yet?

OFFICER: No, not yet, but she'll come soon. Do you know what's behind that door?

BILL-POSTER: No, I've never seen that door open.

OFFICER: I'll telephone for a locksmith to come and open it. [*Goes to the telephone. The* BILL-POSTER *sticks up a poster.*]

DAUGHTER: What was wrong with your net?

BILL-POSTER: Wrong? Well, there wasn't anything actually wrong — but it wasn't as I'd imagined it, so I didn't get so much pleasure from it.

DAUGHTER: How had you imagined the net?

BILL-POSTER: How? That I can't say —

DAUGHTER: Let me tell you. You had imagined it
as it wasn't. Green, yes, but not *that* green.

BILL-POSTER: You know, madam! You know everything
— that's why everyone comes to you with their worries.
If you'd listen to me just once too —

DAUGHTER: Yes, gladly. Come in here, [and tell me
everything] .

> *She goes into her lodge. The* BILL-POSTER *stands
> outside the window and speaks to her. [The stage is
> darkened. When it becomes light, the lime-tree is green
> again, the monk's-hood in flower and the sun is
> shining on the green foliage outside.] The* OFFICER
> *enters. Now he is old, white-haired and shabby, with
> worn-out shoes, and carries the twigs of his rose
> bouquet. He wanders up and down, slowly, like an
> old man. He reads the poster. A* BALLET DANCER
> *enters, right.*

OFFICER: Has Miss Victoria gone?

BALLET DANCER: No, not yet.

OFFICER: Then I'll wait. She'll come soon, won't she?

BALLET DANCER [*earnestly*] : Oh, yes, certainly.

OFFICER: Don't go now, you'll be able to see what's
behind this door, for I've sent for the locksmith.

BALLET DANCER: It'll be really interesting to see that
door opened. That door and the rising castle. Do you
know the rising castle?

OFFICER: Do I know it? I've been a prisoner there.

BALLET DANCER: No, was that you? But why did they
have so many horses there?

OFFICER: It was a cavalry barracks, of course.

BALLET DANCER [*annoyed with herself*]: How stupid I am. Fancy my not realizing that!

   A SINGER *enters right.*

OFFICER: Has Miss Victoria left?

SINGER [*earnestly*]: No, she hasn't left. She never leaves.

OFFICER: That is because she loves me. You mustn't go before the locksmith comes to open this door.

SINGER: Oh, is the door to be opened? What fun! I must just ask the stage-door keeper something —

   PROMPTER *enters right.*

OFFICER: Has Miss Victoria left?

PROMPTER: Not as far as I know.

OFFICER: You see! Didn't I say she was waiting for me? You mustn't go before the door is opened.

PROMPTER: Which door?

OFFICER: Is there more than one door?

PROMPTER: Oh, I know. The one with the clover-leaf. Yes, I'll certainly stay. I must just have a word with the stage-door keeper.

   The BALLET DANCER, SINGER *and* PROMPTER *group themselves beside the* BILL-POSTER *outside the* STAGE-DOOR KEEPER's *window, where in turn they speak to the* DAUGHTER. *The* GLAZIER *enters through the gate.*

OFFICER: Is that the locksmith?

GLAZIER: No, the locksmith was busy. But it can be done as well by a glazier.

OFFICER: Yes, yes, I'm sure. But have you got a diamond?

GLAZIER: Of course. Who ever heard of a glazier without a diamond?

OFFICER: That's true. Then let us get to work! [*He claps his hands. They all gather in a circle around the door.* [SINGERS *dressed as the Mastersingers and* GIRL DANCERS *dressed for Aida run in right.*] Locksmith — or glazier — do your duty! [*The* GLAZIER *comes forward with a diamond.*] A moment such as this does not often recur in a person's life, so, my good friends, I beg you, consider carefully —

POLICEMAN [*enters*]: In the name of the law I forbid the opening of this door!

OFFICER: Oh, God, the trouble whenever one wants to do anything new and big! We'll take it to court. To the advocate! Then we'll see how the law stands. To the advocate!

[*The scene is changed to an* ADVOCATE'S *office. This is done in full view of the audience, thus. The gate remains, serving as part of an entry barrier like a counter which extends the full width of the stage. The* STAGE-DOOR KEEPER'S *hatch remains as the* ADVOCATE'S *nook containing his desk, opening downstage. The lime-tree, leafless, is now a coat and hat stand. The poster hoarding is hung with notices and court papers. The door with the clover-leaf becomes part of a filing cupboard.*

The ADVOCATE, *in morning-coat and white cravat, is seated on the left inside the gate at a desk covered with papers. His face reflects extreme suffering; it is chalk-white and lined, with purple shadows; he is ugly, a mirror of every kind of crime and vice which his profession forces him to experience vicariously. One of his two* CLERKS *is one-armed, the other one-eyed. The characters who have gathered in the preceding scene to see the door opened are still on stage, now as though awaiting admission to the* ADVOCATE, *with the appearance of having been there for ever. The* DAUGHTER *(in her shawl) and the* OFFICER *stand downstage.*]

ADVOCATE [*comes over to the* DAUGHTER]: Please may I have the shawl? I'll hang it in here till I light the stove. Then I'll burn it with all its griefs and sorrows.

DAUGHTER: Not yet, I want to finish it first. And I want to gather up all *your* griefs, the confidences you've received about crimes and vices, unjust imprisonments, slanders, calumnies —

ADVOCATE: My little friend, your shawl would not suffice. Look at these walls. Isn't it as though all these sins had soiled the paper? Look at these documents on which I write accounts of injustices. Look at me. No one ever comes here who laughs. Only hard glances, bared teeth, clenched fists. And they all spray their malice, their envy, their suspicions, over me. Look, my hands are black, and can never be cleansed, do you see how they are cracked and bloody? I can never wear clothes for more than one or two days, because they stink of other men's crimes. Sometimes I have sulphur burned here, but it doesn't help. I sleep in here and dream only of crimes. I've a murder case right now; that I can bear, but do you know what's the worst of all? To part a husband and wife; that makes the earth cry out to heaven, cry treachery against creation, against goodness, against love. And when these briefs are filled with their mutual accusations and at length a humane fellow creature receives one of the two in private, takes him or her by the ear and, smiling, asks the simple question, "What is your real complaint against your husband — or wife?" — then he or she stands there, speechless, unable to answer. Once, yes, it was a question of a green salad, another time a single word, most often it's nothing. But the pain, the suffering! These *I* must endure. Look at me! Do you think I could win a woman's love with this criminal's visage? And do you think anyone wants to be friends with a man who must collect all the city's debts? It is dreadful to be part of mankind.

DAUGHTER: Alas for mankind!

ADVOCATE: Alas indeed. And what people live on is to me a riddle. [They marry on an income of a hundred pounds, when they need two hundred.] They borrow, of course, everyone borrows. They live from day to day and muddle through to death. And they always leave debts behind them. Who will pay in the end, tell me that?

DAUGHTER: He Who feeds the birds.

ADVOCATE: Yes. But if He Who feeds the birds were to step down to His earth and see how His poor children fare, He might perhaps be moved to pity —

DAUGHTER: Alas for mankind!

ADVOCATE: Alas indeed. [*To the* OFFICER.] What do you want?

OFFICER: I only wanted to ask if Miss Victoria has left.

ADVOCATE: No, she hasn't, you may rest assured. Why are you pointing at my cupboard?

OFFICER: I thought that door was so like —

ADVOCATE: Oh, no! No, no!

The church bells ring.

OFFICER: Is there a funeral?

ADVOCATE: No, they're conferring degrees, doctors' degrees. And I must go and be made a Doctor of Law. Perhaps you'd like to become a Doctor and get a laurel crown?

OFFICER: Yes, why not? It'd make a change —

ADVOCATE: Shall we go at once to the great ceremony? Just go and get dressed.

[*The* OFFICER *goes. The stage is darkened, and the scene is changed thus. The barrier remains but now*

*serves as the chancel rail. The poster-hoarding becomes
the number-board for the psalms; the lime-tree/coat-
stand is a candelabra; the* ADVOCATE's *desk serves
for the handing-out of degrees; the clover-leaf door
now leads to the sacristy. The* MASTERSINGERS
become heralds with sceptres, the GIRL DANCERS
are holding laurel wreaths; the OTHERS *stand around
as spectators. The curtain rises revealing a mighty
church organ with a keyboard beneath and a mirror
above.] Music. At the side, the four faculties of
philosophy, theology, medicine and law.*

　　[*After a moment the* HERALDS *enter right
followed by the* DANCERS *holding their laurel
wreaths before them at arm's length.] Three*
RECIPIENTS OF DEGREES *enter left, one after the
other, and are crowned with wreaths by the* DANCERS;
then they go out right. The ADVOCATE *goes up to
be crowned, but the* DANCERS *turn away, refusing to
crown him, and go out. The* ADVOCATE, *crushed,
leans against a pillar. Everyone goes out, leaving the*
ADVOCATE *alone.*

[DAUGHTER [*enters with a white shawl over her head and
shoulders*]: Look, now I've washed the shawl. But why
are you standing here? Didn't you get the wreath?]

ADVOCATE: [No.] I was unworthy.

DAUGHTER: Why? Because you embraced the cause of
the poor, said a good word for the criminal, lightened the
burden of the guilty, won reprieves for the condemned.
[Alas for mankind. They are not angels; but they are much
to be pitied.]

ADVOCATE: Speak no evil of mankind. I shall plead its
cause.

DAUGHTER: Why do they strike their friends in the face?

ADVOCATE: They know no better.

[DAUGHTER: Let us enlighten them. Will you? With me?

ADVOCATE: They will not accept enlightenment. Oh, if only our complaints could reach the gods in heaven!

DAUGHTER: They shall. [*At the organ.*] Do you know what I see in this mirror? The world set to rights. It is twisted out of true.

ADVOCATE: How did it become so?

DAUGHTER: When the copy was made.

ADVOCATE: Yes. The copy. I always felt that it was a false copy. And when I began to think of the prototype, I realized its inadequacy. People called it human insatiability, the glass splinter that Satan sets in human eyes, and so forth —

DAUGHTER: Their vision is certainly distorted. Look at these university faculties! The government, in order to keep society stable, pays lip service to all four of them. Theology, the teaching of God, which is always attacked and ridiculed by philosophy, which claims to be wisdom itself! And medicine, which challenges philosophy and says that theology is no science but a superstition. And they sit in the same senate, which is supposed to teach the young respect — for the university! It's a madhouse. And alas for him who first sees the truth!

ADVOCATE: The first to see it are the theologians. As part of their preliminary studies they read philosophy, which teaches them that theology is nonsense. Then they read in their theology that philosophy is nonsense. Madmen, eh?

DAUGHTER: And law — the servant of all, except the servants.

ADVOCATE: Justice which, seeking to be just, slays itself. Right, that so often causes wrong.

DAUGHTER: Thus have you arranged your world, child of man. Come — I will give you a wreath which will suit you better. [*Places a crown of thorns on his head.*] Now I will play for you.

> *She sits at the organ and plays a Kyrie, but instead of the music, human voices are heard.*

CHILDREN'S VOICES: Eternal One! Eternal One! [*The last note is prolonged.*]

WOMEN'S VOICES: Have mercy! [*The last note is prolonged.*]

MEN'S VOICES(TENORS): Save us, for Thy mercy's sake! [*The last note is prolonged.*]

MEN'S VOICES (BASSES): Spare Thy children, O lord, and be not wrathful with us!

ALL: Have mercy! Hear us! Pity us mortals! Eternal One, why hast Thou forsaken us? From the deep we beseech Thee: mercy, O Eternal One! Place not too heavy a burden on Thy children. Hear us! Hear us!

> *The stage is darkened. The* DAUGHTER *rises and goes towards the* ADVOCATE. *The organ is transformed by a change of lighting into Fingal's Cave. The sea rolls in beneath the basalt columns. We hear the sound of wind and waves.*

ADVOCATE: What do you hear, sister?

DAUGHTER: What do you hear?

ADVOCATE: I hear raindrops falling.

DAUGHTER: They are the tears of humans weeping. What else do you hear?

ADVOCATE: Sighing — wailing — mourning.]

DAUGHTER[: Mankind's complaints have reached here. They reach no further.] But why this eternal lamentation? Has life no cause for joy?

ADVOCATE: Yes, the fairest of things, which is the bitterest: love. A wife and a home; the best thing, and the worst.

DAUGHTER: I shall try it.

ADVOCATE: With me?

DAUGHTER: With you. You know the rocks, the reefs. We shall avoid them.

ADVOCATE: I am poor.

DAUGHTER: What of that, if we love each other? And a little beauty costs nothing.

ADVOCATE: I hate things which you may love.

DAUGHTER: Then we must compromise.

ADVOCATE: If we tire of each other?

DAUGHTER: Then a child will come and give us a happiness which will never fade.

ADVOCATE: You want me, poor and ugly, despised, an outcast?

AGNES: Yes. [Let us unite our faults.]

ADVOCATE: So be it, then.

A very simple room in the ADVOCATE's *office. Right, a large double bed beneath a canopy and curtains. By it, a window. Left, an iron stove with saucepans, etc.* KRISTIN *is pasting the inside window-joints.* [*Upstage, an open door to the office, where poor people can be seen waiting for an audience.*]

KRISTIN: I'm pasting, I'm pasting.

DAUGHTER [*pale and haggard, sits by the stove*]: You're shutting out the air. I'm suffocating.

KRISTIN: Now there's only one little crack left.

DAUGHTER: [Air, air!] I can't breathe!

KRISTIN: I'm pasting, I'm pasting!

ADVOCATE: That's right, Kristin. Heat costs money.

DAUGHTER: Oh, it's as though you were pasting my lips together!

ADVOCATE [*in the doorway with a document in his hand*]: Is the child asleep?

DAUGHTER: Yes, at last.

ADVOCATE [*gently*]: His cries scare away my clients.

DAUGHTER [*gently*]: What can we do about it?

ADVOCATE: Nothing.

DAUGHTER: We must find a bigger apartment.

ADVOCATE: We have no money.

DAUGHTER: May I open the window? This air is stifling me.

ADVOCATE: Then the heat will go and we shall freeze.

DAUGHTER: It's horrible. May we scrub the floor out there, then?

ADVOCATE: You haven't the strength, nor have I, and Kristin — Kristin must paste. She must paste the whole house tight, every crack in the ceilings, the floors, the walls.

DAUGHTER: Poverty I was prepared for, but not dirt.

ADVOCATE: Poverty is always more or less dirty.

DAUGHTER: This is worse than I had dreamed.

ADVOCATE: We're not too badly off. There's still food in the pot.

DAUGHTER: But what food!

ADVOCATE: Cabbage is cheap, nourishing and good.

DAUGHTER: If you like cabbage. It revolts me.

ADVOCATE: Why didn't you say so?

DAUGHTER: Because I loved you. I wanted to make a sacrifice for you.

ADVOCATE: Then I must sacrifice for you my love of cabbage. The sacrifice must be mutual.

DAUGHTER: Then what shall we eat? Fish? But you hate fish.

ADVOCATE: And it's dear.

DAUGHTER: This is harder than I had dreamed.

ADVOCATE [*gently*]: You see how hard it is! And the child, that was to have been our bond and our blessing, is becoming our ruin.

DAUGHTER: My dearest! I am dying in this air, in this room with its window on the yard, the child's ceaseless crying so that I can never sleep, the people out there with their complainings, strifes and accusations. I must die if I stay here.

ADVOCATE: Poor little flower. No light, no air —

DAUGHTER: And you say there are some who are worse off.

ADVOCATE: Many of the neighbours envy me.

DAUGHTER: I could bear it if only I could have a little beauty in my home.

ADVOCATE: I know you mean a flower, if possible a heliotrope, but that costs a shilling, and that's twelve pints of milk or four pounds of potatoes.

DAUGHTER: I'll gladly do without food if I may have my flower.

ADVOCATE: There is a kind of beauty which costs nothing,

and whose absence from a home is the worst torment for a man who loves beauty.

DAUGHTER: What is that?

ADVOCATE: If I say, you will be angry.

DAUGHTER: We have agreed not to be angry.

ADVOCATE: We have agreed. Everything will be all right, Agnes, as long as we don't speak sharply. You know what I mean. Not yet!

DAUGHTER: We shall never do that.

ADVOCATE: I never shall.

DAUGHTER: Tell me, now.

ADVOCATE: Well. When I enter a home I first look to see how the curtain sits on its rail. [*Goes over to the window and adjusts the curtain.*] If it hangs like a rope or a rag, I leave. Then I glance at the chairs. If they stand straight, I stay. [*Adjusts a chair against the wall.*] Then I look at the candles in their sticks. If they are crooked, the whole house is awry. [*Corrects a candle on the desk.*] This is the beauty, you see, my dear, that costs nothing.

DAUGHTER [*drops her head*]: Don't speak so sharply, Axel.

ADVOCATE: I was not speaking sharply.

DAUGHTER: Yes, you were.

ADVOCATE: Look, for God's sake — !

DAUGHTER: What kind of language is that?

ADVOCATE: Forgive me, Agnes. But I have suffered from your untidiness as much as you suffer from dirt. And I haven't dared to tidy things up myself, because then you get angry as though I had reproached you. Ugh! Shall we stop now?

[DAUGHTER: It is horribly difficult to be married. The most difficult thing of all. I think one has to be an angel.

ADVOCATE: Yes. I agree.]

DAUGHTER: I think I shall begin to hate you after this.

ADVOCATE: No, Agnes. Let us beware of hatred. I promise I shall never remark on your untidiness again — though it tortures me.

DAUGHTER: And I shall eat cabbage, though it tortures me.

ADVOCATE: We must torture each other, then. What makes one happy, torments the other.

DAUGHTER: Alas for mankind!

ADVOCATE: You see it now?

DAUGHTER: Yes. But let us in God's name avoid these reefs, now we know them so well.

ADVOCATE: Let us do that. We are humane and enlightened people. We can forgive and forget.

DAUGHTER: We can smile at such trifles.

ADVOCATE: We can — *we* can! Do you know, I read in the paper this morning — by the way, where is the paper?

DAUGHTER [*embarrassed*]: Which paper?

ADVOCATE [*harshly*]: Do I take more than one paper?

DAUGHTER: Smile now, and don't reproach me. I used your paper to make the fire.

ADVOCATE [*angrily*]: For God's sake!

DAUGHTER: Smile, now. I burned it because he mocked what is sacred to me —

ADVOCATE: And what is not sacred to me. Well! [*Clasps his hands, furious.*] I shall smile, I shall smile so that my back teeth show. I shall be humane, and sweep my opinions under the carpet, and say yes to everything and act the hypocrite. So, you've burned my newspaper. I see. [*Adjusts the curtain by the bedpost.*] Now I'm tidying things again, and you'll be angry. Agnes, this is impossible.

DAUGHTER: Yes, yes.

ADVOCATE: But we must go on, not because of our vows, but for the child.

DAUGHTER: That's right. For the child. Oh — oh — we must go on.

ADVOCATE: And now I must go out to my clients. Listen, they're buzzing with impatience to get at each other's throats, have each other fined and imprisoned. Lost souls — !

DAUGHTER: Unhappy people. And this pasting! [*Bows her head in silent despair.*]

KRISTIN: I'm pasting, I'm pasting!

The ADVOCATE *stands at the door and fingers the latch nervously.*

DAUGHTER: Oh, how that latch squeaks! It's as though you were squeezing my heart's springs —

ADVOCATE: I'm squeezing, I'm squeezing —

DAUGHTER: Don't do it!

ADVOCATE: I'm squeezing!

DAUGHTER: No!

ADVOCATE: I'm — !

OFFICER [*enters from the office, puts his hand on the latch*] : Allow me.

ADVOCATE [*lets go of the latch*] : Certainly. Since you are now a Doctor.

OFFICER: Now life lies before me! All paths stand open to me, my feet are on Parnassus, I have won my laurels, immortality, honour. [Everything is mine.]

ADVOCATE: What will you live on?

OFFICER: Live on?

ADVOCATE: You must have a home, clothes, food?

OFFICER: That always works out, if only one has someone who loves one.

ADVOCATE: Perhaps. Perhaps. Paste, Kristin! Paste! Till they can't breathe. [*Goes out backwards, nodding.*]

KRISTIN: I'm pasting, I'm pasting! Till they can't breathe.

OFFICER [*to* DAUGHTER]: Will you come with me now?

DAUGHTER: At once. But where?

OFFICER: To Fairhaven! There it is summer, there the sun shines, there are young people, children and flowers, singing and dancing, feasting and joy!

DAUGHTER: Then I want to go there.

OFFICER: Come, come!

ADVOCATE [*enters again*]: Now I am returning to my first hell. This was the second — and the worst. The greatest happiness is the greatest hell. Now she's dropped hairpins on the floor again. [*Picks around on the floor.*]

OFFICER: Fancy, now he's found the hairpins too.

ADVOCATE: Too? Look at this one. Here are two prongs, but one pin. It is two, but it is one. If I straighten it out it is a single entity. If I bend it, it is two without ceasing to be one. That means: these two are one. But if I break it — so! Now they are two, two! [*Breaks the hairpin and throws the pieces away.*]

OFFICER: All this he has seen. But before one can break it, the prongs must diverge. If they converge, then it will hold.

ADVOCATE: And if they are parallel, then they never meet. They will neither hold nor break.

OFFICER: The hairpin is the most complete of all created things. A straight line which is identical with two parallels.

ADVOCATE: A lock which fastens when it is open.

OFFICER: Clasping a plait of hair, whose ends stay open when it is clasped shut.

ADVOCATE: Like this door. When I shut it, I open, the way out, for you, Agnes. [*Goes out and shuts the door.*]

OFFICER: Shall we go, then?

[*The scene changes. The bed with its canopy and curtains becomes a tent. The iron stove remains; the backcloth is raised, and we see, in the right foreground, scorched mountains with red heather and black and white stumps of trees left by a forest fire. Red pigsties and outhouses. Below stands an open gymnasium for the sick, with people exercising on machines resembling instruments of torture. Downstage left are some open sheds of the quarantine building, with ovens, furnace rooms and pipes. Centre stage, a broad sea channel. Upstage, a beautiful beach with trees, and jetties decked with flags. White boats are moored to them, some with sails set, some not. Small Italian villas, pavilions, kiosks and marble statues can be seen through the trees.*] The QUARANTINE MASTER *is walking on the beach dressed as a blackamoor.*

OFFICER [*enters and shakes the* QUARANTINE MASTER's *hand*]: Why, Ordström! Have you landed here?

QUARANTINE MASTER: Yes, I'm here.

OFFICER: Is this Fairhaven?

QUARANTINE MASTER: No, that's on the other side. This is Foulstrand.

OFFICER: Then we've come wrong.

QUARANTINE MASTER: We? Won't you introduce me?

OFFICER: No, that wouldn't be proper. [*Whispers.*] This is Indra's own daughter!

QUARANTINE MASTER: Indra's? I thought it was Waruna herself. Well, aren't you surprised I'm black in the face?

OFFICER: My son, I am fifty years old, and then one is no longer surprised. I assumed immediately that you were going to a masked ball this evening.

QUARANTINE MASTER: Quite right. And I hope you will join me?

OFFICER: By all means. This place — doesn't look tempting. What kind of people live here?

QUARANTINE MASTER: The sick ones live here, the healthy over there.

OFFICER: There are only poor people here, then?

QUARANTINE MASTER: No, my lad, these are the rich ones. Look at that fellow [on the rack there]. He's eaten too much *foie gras* with truffles and drunk so much Burgundy that his feet have become like briar-wood.

OFFICER: Briar-wood?

QUARANTINE MASTER: Yes. He's got briar-wood feet. And that fellow [lying on the guillotine]. He's drunk so much brandy they had to run his spine through the mangle.

OFFICER: That's not good either.

QUARANTINE MASTER: Everyone lives here who has some grief to hide. Look at him, for instance.

An OLD DANDY *is wheeled in in a wheel-chair, accompanied by a sixty-year-old scrawny ugly* COQUETTE, *dressed in the latest mode, and herself accompanied by a* MALE "FRIEND" *of forty.*

OFFICER: It's the Major! Our old schoolfellow!

QUARANTINE MASTER: Don Juan! You see, he's still in love with that spook at his side. He doesn't see that she's grown old, that she's ugly, faithless, cruel.

OFFICER: There's love for you. I'd never have believed that lecher could love so deeply and sincerely.

QUARANTINE MASTER: You're very charitable.

OFFICER: I myself have loved Victoria. Yes, I still walk the corridor and wait for her —

QUARANTINE MASTER: Is it you who walks in the corridor?

OFFICER: It is I.

QUARANTINE MASTER: Well, have you opened the door yet?

OFFICER: No, it's still *sub judice*. The bill-poster is out with his fishing-net, of course, so they're held up for evidence. Meanwhile the glazier has put the windows in at the castle, which has risen half a storey. It's been an uncommonly fine year this year. Warm and damp.

QUARANTINE MASTER: But you've never been as warm as it is where I work.

OFFICER: How hot is it in the ovens, then?

QUARANTINE MASTER: When we disinfect cholera suspects, we bring it up to a hundred and thirty.

OFFICER: Is the cholera loose again now?

QUARANTINE MASTER: Don't you know?

OFFICER: Yes, of course I know, but I so often forget what I know.

QUARANTINE MASTER: I often wish I could forget, especially myself. That's why I go to masquerades, fancy-dress balls and social occasions.

OFFICER: Why, what have you done?

QUARANTINE MASTER: If I talk about it they say I'm boasting, if I keep quiet they call me a hypocrite.

OFFICER: Is that why you've blacked your face?

QUARANTINE MASTER: Yes. A little blacker than I really am.

OFFICER: Who is that coming now?

QUARANTINE MASTER: Oh, some poet who needs a mud-bath.

The POET *enters, glancing at the sky, with a bucket of mud in his hand.*

OFFICER: Mud? Surely he needs light and air!

QUARANTINE MASTER: No, he always lives miles up in space, so he gets nostalgic for mud. It makes your skin hard like a pig's to roll in mud. Then he doesn't feel the gadfly's sting.

[OFFICER: This curious world of contradictions!]

POET [*ecstatically*]: Out of clay the god Ptah created man on a potter's wheel, a lathe. [*Sceptically.*] Or some other damned thing! [*Ecstatically.*] From clay the sculptor creates his more or less immortal masterpieces. [*Sceptically.*] Which are usually just crap! [*Ecstatically.*] From clay are created those indispensable kitchen utensils which men call by the common names of pots and plates. [*Sceptically.*] What the hell do I care what they're called? [*Ecstatically.*] Such is clay! When clay is liquid they call it mud. *C'est mon affaire!* [*Shouts.*] Lina!

LINA *enters with a bucket.*

POET: Lina, show yourself to Miss Agnes. She knew you ten years ago when you were a young, happy and we may say beautiful girl. See how she is now! Five children, drudgery, squalling, starvation, ironing! See how her beauty has gone, how her joy has vanished, through the performance of those duties which should have given her that inner happiness which expresses itself in the harmony of the facial lines and the still glow of the eyes —

QUARANTINE MASTER [*puts his hand over the* POET's *mouth*]: Stuff it, stuff it.

POET: That's what they all say. And if one is silent, then they say: "Speak!" Impossible creatures.

DAUGHTER [*goes over to* LINA]: Let me hear your complaint.

LINA: No, I daren't. Or he'll make things worse.

DAUGHTER: Who is so cruel?

LINA: I daren't say, or I'll get beaten.

POET: That's the way it is. [But I'll tell you, even if this blackamoor knocks my teeth out. Let me inform you that injustices sometimes occur. Agnes, daughter of God! Do you hear music and dancing from the hillside up there? Well, that is Lina's sister, who has come home from the city, where she — went astray, if you understand me? Now they are killing the fatted calf, but Lina who stayed at home has to carry the swill and feed the pigs.

DAUGHTER: They rejoice because the prodigal has ceased from her straying, not simply because she has come home. Remember that.

POET: Very well. But then put on a dance and a supper each evening for this irreproachable working-girl who has never strayed! Do that. But they won't do it. When Lina isn't working she has to go to church to be reproached for not being perfect. Is this justice?

DAUGHTER: Your questions are so difficult to answer, because — there are so many things one can't foresee —

POET: That was also the opinion of the Caliph, Haroun the Just. He sat still on his throne and never saw from up there what went on down below. In the end their com-

plaints reached his lofty ear. Then one fine day he
stepped down, disguised himself and walked unobserved
among his people to see what had gone wrong with his
justice.

DAUGHTER: Surely you don't think I am Haroun the Just?

OFFICER: Let's talk about something else. Look, we've
got visitors.

> *A white boat shaped like a dragon with a sail of light-
> blue silk on a golden yard, and a gilded mast with a
> rose-red pennant, glides across the water from the
> left. At the rudder, closely entwined, sit* HE *and* SHE.

OFFICER: Look at that. Perfect happiness, unqualified
bliss. The joy of young love.]

HE [*stands up in the boat and sings*]:
>   Hail to thee, Fairhaven,
>   Where once I saw the spring.
>   Where I dreamed my first, fair dreams.
>   Here I am again!
>   Not alone as then.
>   Groves and bays,
>   Sky and sea,
>   Greet her, my love, my bride,
>   My sun, my life!

> [*The flags on the jetties of Fairhaven greet them.
> White handkerchieves wave from the villas and the
> beaches, and a harmony of harps and violins rings
> out across the water.*

POET: See what a light shines from them! Hear how the
sea resounds with music! Such is Love.]

OFFICER: It is Victoria!

QUARANTINE MASTER: Well?

OFFICER: It is his Victoria. I have mine. And mine, no
one may see. [Raise the quarantine flag now, and I'll
pull in the net.]

The QUARANTINE MASTER *waves a yellow flag.*
[*The* OFFICER *pulls a rope so that the boat swings
towards Foulstrand.*] HE *and* SHE *become aware of
the horrible landscape and grimace with disgust.*

QUARANTINE MASTER: Yes, yes! It isn't nice. But
everyone must come here, everyone who has been contaminated.

[POET: Imagine being able to talk like that, to do such
things, when one sees two people in love! Don't touch
them! Don't touch Love! It's *lèse-majesté*! Alas, alas!
Now all that is beautiful must be debased, hauled down
into the mud!

HE *and* SHE *step ashore, downcast and ashamed.*]

HE: What have we done?

QUARANTINE MASTER: You don't need to have done
anything to be contaminated by the petty dirt of life.

[SHE: So short is happiness and joy!]

HE: How long must we stay here?

QUARANTINE MASTER: Forty days and nights.

[SHE: Then we'd rather go back.]

HE: Live here, among scorched hills and pigsties?

POET: Love conquers all, even sulphur and carbolic.

QUARANTINE MASTER [*lights the oven. Blue sulphur
fumes arise*] : Now I'm lighting the sulphur. Please step
inside.

SHE: Oh! My blue dress will lose its colour.

QUARANTINE MASTER: And turn white. Your red
roses shall also turn white.

HE: And your cheeks. Forty days!

SHE [*to the* OFFICER] That will please you.

OFFICER: No, it will not. Your joy was the cause of my grief, but — it doesn't matter — I am now a Doctor and have a standing over there [on the mainland.] Ho, ho, yes, yes. And in the autumn I shall get a place in a school — to read with schoolboys the lessons I learned in my childhood and youth, and must learn now, the same lessons, throughout my manhood and my old age, the same lessons . . . How much is two times two? How many times does two go into four? Till they retire me and I can go — jobless, waiting for mealtimes and newspapers, — until at last they carry me out to the crematorium and burn me up. Have you no pensioners out here? That must be the worst thing after twice two is four: to start school again, when you've got your Doctorate; to ask the same questions until you die. [An OLD MAN walks by with his hands behind his back.] Look, there goes a pensioner, waiting for death; doubtless a captain who never became a major, or a high-court clerk who never rose to be judge. Many are called, but few are chosen. He's waiting for his lunch —

PENSIONER: No, for my paper! My morning paper!

OFFICER: And he's only fifty-four. He may live twenty-five more years waiting for his meals and his paper. Isn't it horrible?

PENSIONER: What isn't horrible? Answer me, answer!

OFFICER: Yes, answer who can. Now I must study with schoolboys; twice two is four! How many times does two go into four? [Clasps his head desperately.] Oh, Victoria, whom I loved, and therefore wished all happiness on earth — now she has happiness, the best she can imagine, and I suffer — suffer —suffer!

SHE: Do you think I can be happy, when I see you suffer? How can you think that? Perhaps it soothes your pain that I must sit imprisoned here for forty days and nights? Tell me, does that soothe your pain?

OFFICER: Yes and no. I cannot be happy while you suffer. Ah!

[HE: And do you think my happiness can be built on your suffering?

OFFICER: Alas for us all!

ALL [*stretch their hands towards heaven and emit a discordant cry of pain*] : Ah!]

DAUGHTER:[Eternal One, hear them! Life is cruel!] Alas for mankind!

[ALL[*as before*] : Ah!

> *For a moment the stage is darkened. Everyone either goes out, or moves to another position. When it becomes light again, we see the shore of Foulstrand, upstage but in shadow. The water still occupies the centre stage; downstage is Fairhaven; both are fully illuminated. Right, the corner of a casino, with windows open, through which can be seen couples dancing. On an empty packing-case outside stand* THREE GIRLS, *their arms round each others' waists, watching the dancing. On the steps of the casino is a bench on which* UGLY EDITH *sits, bare-headed and sad, her hair a dishevelled mass. Before her stands a piano, its keyboard open. Left, a yellow wooden house.* TWO CHILDREN *in summer dress are throwing a ball outside.*
>
> *At the rear of the foreground is a jetty, with white boats and flagpoles with flags. Out in the water is a white man-of-war, rigged brig-fashion, with cannon portholes. But the whole landscape is in winter dress, with snow on the ground and on the leafless trees.*
>
> *The* DAUGHTER *and the* OFFICER *enter.*]

DAUGHTER: Here is the peace and joy of holiday. Work has stopped. They have parties every day. The people walk in holiday clothes. They play and dance even in the mornings. [[*To the* CHILDREN.] Why don't you go inside and dance, children?

CHILDREN: Us?

OFFICER: But they are servants.

DAUGHTER: Oh, yes.] But why is Edith sitting there instead of inside?

EDITH *hides her face in her hands.*

OFFICER: Don't ask her. She has been sitting there for three hours and no one has asked her to dance. [[*He goes into the yellow house, left.*]]

DAUGHTER: What a cruel pastime!

MOTHER [*enters, bare-necked, goes over to* EDITH]: Why don't you go inside as I told you?

EDITH: Because — I can't offer myself. I'm ugly, I know that, so no one will dance with me, but I don't need to be reminded of it by you.

> *She begins to play the piano:* [*Bach's Toccata and Fugue, opus 10. The waltz from inside the casino is heard, at first softly, then louder, as though competing with the Bach. But* EDITH *plays louder and silences the dance music.* GUESTS *appear in the doorway and listen to her playing. Everyone on stage stands devoutly listening.*]

A NAVAL OFFICER [*takes* ALICE, *one of the guests at the ball, round the waist and leads her down to the jetty*]: Come, quickly!

> EDITH *stops playing, gets up and looks at them in despair. She remains standing like a statue.* [*The wall of the yellow house is removed and*] *we see three school benches, with* SCHOOLBOYS *sitting on them. Amongst them is the* OFFICER, *looking ill-at-ease and worried. The* SCHOOLMASTER, *with spectacles, chalk and a cane, stands facing them.*

SCHOOLMASTER [*to the* OFFICER]: Well, my boy, can you tell me what two times two is? [*The* OFFICER *remains seated, searching his memory painfully without finding the answer.*] Stand up when you're asked a question.

OFFICER [*gets up miserably*] : Two times two. Let me see. It is two two!

SCHOOLMASTER: I see. You haven't done your homework.

OFFICER [*ashamed*] : Yes, I have, but — I don't know why, but I can't say it.

SCHOOLMASTER: You're making excuses! You know, but you can't say it? Perhaps I can help you. [*Pulls the OFFICER's hair.*]

OFFICER: Oh, this is dreadful, it's dreadful.

SCHOOLMASTER: Yes, it's dreadful that such a big boy has no ambition —

OFFICER [*in torment*] : A big boy, yes, I am big, much bigger than them. I'm a Doctor. Why am I sitting here? Aren't I a Doctor?

SCHOOLMASTER: You are, but you must sit and mature, you see. You must mature. Isn't that right?

OFFICER [*clutches his forehead*] : Yes, that's right, one must mature. Two times two — is two, and I can prove that by analogy, the highest of all forms of proof. Listen now. One times one is one, so two times two must be two. For what applies to one must apply to the other.

SCHOOLMASTER: Your proof obeys the law of logic, but your answer is incorrect.

OFFICER: What obeys the law of logic cannot be incorrect. Let us try. One into one goes once, so two into two goes twice.

SCHOOLMASTER: Quite correct, according to your analogy. But then, how much is one times three?

OFFICER: It is three!

SCHOOLMASTER: Then two times three must also be three.

OFFICER [*reflectively*]: No, that can't be right. It can't. Unless — ! [*Sits down in despair.*] No, I'm not mature yet.

SCHOOLMASTER: No, not by a long way.

OFFICER: But how long must I sit here, then?

SCHOOLMASTER: How long here? Do you think that time and space exist? Suppose that time exists, then you must be able to say what time is. What is time?

OFFICER: Time. [*Thinks.*] That I can't say, but I know what it is; therefore I can know how much two times two is without being able to say it. Can you tell me what time is?

SCHOOLMASTER: Of course I can.

OFFICER [*and all the class*]: Say, then.

SCHOOLMASTER: Time? Let me see. [*Stands motionless with his finger to his nose.*] While we talk, time runs. So, time is something that runs while I talk.

A BOY [*gets up*]: You're talking now, and while you talk I run; so I am time. [*Runs out.*]

SCHOOLMASTER: That is perfectly correct, according to the laws of logic.

OFFICER: But then the laws of logic are insane, for Nils who ran away cannot be time.

SCHOOLMASTER: That is also perfectly correct according to the laws of logic, although it is insane.

OFFICER: Then logic is insane.

SCHOOLMASTER: It certainly seems so. But if logic is insane the whole world is insane, and why should I sit here and teach you insanities? Let's find a bottle and have a drink and a swim.

OFFICER: This is *posterius prius,* time reversed. People swim first and drink afterwards. You old duffer!

SCHOOLMASTER: Now, Doctor, don't be impertinent.

OFFICER: Lieutenant, if you don't mind. I am an officer, and I don't understand why I'm sitting here being scolded among schoolboys —

SCHOOLMASTER [*raises a finger*] : We must mature!

QUARANTINE MASTER [*enters*] : The quarantine's starting! The quarantine's starting!

OFFICER: Oh, there you are. Can you imagine, this fellow makes me sit on a school bench, although I'm a Doctor.

QUARANTINE MASTER: Well, why don't you get up and go?

OFFICER: What? Go? I can't do that.

SCHOOLMASTER: I should think not. Just you try.

OFFICER [*to* QUARANTINE MASTER] : Save me! Save me from his eyes!

QUARANTINE MASTER: Come along. Come and help us dance. We must dance before the plague breaks out. We must!

[OFFICER: Will the warship sail then?

QUARANTINE MASTER: It will sail first. And then there'll be tears.

OFFICER: Always tears. When he comes, and when he goes. Let us go.

> They go. The SCHOOLMASTER *silently continues with his lesson.*
>
> The YOUNG GIRLS, *who were standing at the window of the ballroom, go sadly down to the jetty.*

EDITH, *who has been standing as though petrified at the piano, follows them.*

DAUGHTER: Is no one happy in this Paradise?

OFFICER: Yes, there are two who are newly wed. Listen to them!

A NEWLY MARRIED COUPLE *enter.*

THE HUSBAND [*to his* WIFE]: I am so happy that I should like to die.

WIFE: Why die?

HUSBAND: Because in the midst of my happiness there grows a seed of sadness. It consumes itself like fire. It cannot burn eternally, but must die. This foreboding of the end destroys my happiness at its peak.

WIFE: Let us die together, now.

HUSBAND: Die? Yes! I am frightened of happiness. The betrayer!

They go towards the sea.

DAUGHTER: Life is cruel. Alas for mankind!]

OFFICER: Look at this man! He is the most envied of all who live here. [*The* BLIND MAN *is led in.*] He owns these hundred Italian villas; he owns all these bays, inlets beaches, forests, the fish in the water, the birds in the air and the game in the woods. These thousand people are his tenants and the sun rises over his seas and sinks over his lands —

DAUGHTER: Does he complain too?

OFFICER: Yes, and with reason, for he cannot see.

QUARANTINE MASTER: He is blind.

DAUGHTER: The most envied of all!

OFFICER: Now he wants to see the ship sail out, with his son on board.

BLIND MAN: I do not see, but I hear. I hear how the anchor claws the sea-bed as when one draws the hook from a fish and the heart follows up through the throat. My son, my only child, is going abroad across the wide sea. I can accompany him only in my thoughts. Now I hear the cable screech, and — something flutters and swishes like clothes drying on a line — wet handkerchieves, perhaps — and I hear how it snuffles and sobs, like people crying — perhaps the small waves lapping against the nets, or is it the girls on the shore, the abandoned, the comfortless? Once I asked a child why the sea was salt, and the child who had a father at sea replied at once: "The sea is salt because sailors cry so much." "Why do sailors cry so much?" "Oh," said the child, "because they are always having to go away. That's why they always dry their handkerchieves up on the masts." "Why do people cry when they are sad?" I asked him. "Oh," said the child, "because their eyes have to be washed sometimes so that they can see more clearly."

[*The ship has set sail and glides away. The* GIRLS *on the shore wave their handkerchieves and dab away their tears. On the foremast the signal "Yes" is raised, a red ball on a white background.* ALICE *waves joyfully in reply.*]

DAUGHTER [*to* OFFICER]: What does that flag mean?

OFFICER: It means yes. That is the lieutenant's "Yes" in red, like the red heart's blood drawn on the blue cloth of heaven.

DAUGHTER: How does "No" look, then?

OFFICER: It is blue, like the spoiled blood in his veins. But see how happy Alice is!

DAUGHTER: And how Edith is crying.

THE BLIND MAN: Meeting and parting. Parting and meeting. That is life. I met his mother. And then she went away. I kept our son. Now he is going.

DAUGHTER: He will surely come back.

BLIND MAN: Who is that? I have heard that voice before, in my dreams, in my youth, when the summer holidays began, in the first year of marriage when my child was born. Every time life smiled, I heard that voice.[like the whisper of a breeze from the south, like the music of harps from above, as I imagine the angels to have welcomed Christ on Christmas night.]

   The ADVOCATE *enters, goes over to the* BLIND MAN *and whispers.*

BLIND MAN: I see.

ADVOCATE: Yes, they've eloped. [*Goes over to* DAUGHTER.] Now you have seen almost everything, but you haven't experienced the worst thing.

DAUGHTER: What can that be?

ADVOCATE: Repetition. Repeating the pattern. Go back! Learn your lesson again. Come.

DAUGHTER: Where?

ADVOCATE: To your duties.

DAUGHTER: What is duty?

ADVOCATE: It is everything you shrink from. Everything you don't want to do and must. It is to abstain, to renounce, to go without, to leave behind. Everything unpleasant, repulsive, tedious —

DAUGHTER: Are there no pleasant duties?

ADVOCATE: They become pleasant when you have performed them —

DAUGHTER: When they no longer exist. So duty is always unpleasant. What is pleasant?

ADVOCATE: Sin is pleasant.

DAUGHTER: Sin?

ADVOCATE: Which must be punished, yes. If I have had a pleasant day and evening, I suffer the pangs of hell and a sick conscience the next day.

[DAUGHTER: How strange!]

ADVOCATE: Yes, I wake up in the morning with a head-ache; and then the repetition begins, but a perverse repetition. In such a way that everything that the previous evening was beautiful, pleasant, witty, appears this morning in my memory as ugly, repulsive, stupid. The pleasure rots, and the joy crumbles. What people call success is always the prelude to one's next setback. My successes became my defeat. People have an instinctive fear of other men's successes; they think it unjust that fate should favour one man, so they try to restore the balance by setting rocks in their path. To have talent is dangerous. [One can easily starve to death.] However, go back to your duties, or I shall sue you, and we shall go through all the three courts, one, two, three.

DAUGHTER: Go back? To the iron stove with the pot of cabbage, the child's nappies — ?

ADVOCATE: Yes. Today is washing day. We must wash all the handkerchieves —

DAUGHTER: Oh, must I do all that again?

ADVOCATE: Life consists of doing things again. Look at the schoolmaster in there. Yesterday he got his Doctorate, was crowned with laurel to the sound of cannon, ascended Parnassus and was embraced by the King. And today he starts school again, asks what is two times two, and so he must continue until he dies. [But come back, to your home.

DAUGHTER: I would rather die.

ADVOCATE: Die? One may not. Firstly, because it is dishonourable, so much so that even one's dead body is condemned to insult, and secondly — because it dis-qualifies us from grace. It is a mortal sin.

DAUGHTER: It is not easy to be a human being.

ALL: True!

DAUGHTER: I shall not return to that dirt and degradation with you. I want to return whence I came, but — first I must open the door that I may know the secret. I want the door to be opened!

ADVOCATE: Then you must retrace your steps, return by the same path, and endure all the horrors of trial, the repetitions, the repetitions, the repetitions —

DAUGHTER: So be it. But first I must go alone into the desert to rediscover myself. We shall meet again. [*To the* POET.] Come with me.

> *From the rear of the stage are heard distant cries of anguish.*

DAUGHTER: What was that?

ADVOCATE: The unhappy people of Foulstrand.

DAUGHTER: Why do they cry so much more piteously today?

ADVOCATE: Because the sun is shining here, because here there is music, dancing and youth. It enhances their suffering.

DAUGHTER: We must free them.

ADVOCATE: Try. Someone tried once, and they hanged Him on a cross.

DAUGHTER: Who did?

ADVOCATE: All right-thinking people.

DAUGHTER: Who are they?

ADVOCATE: Don't you know all right-thinking people? Well, you must meet some.

DAUGHTER: Was it they who refused you your laurel wreath?

ADVOCATE: Yes.

DAUGHTER: Then I do know them.

> *A shore by the Mediterranean. Downstage left is a
> white wall, with orange trees in fruit visible over the
> top of it. Upstage, villas and a terraced casino. Right,
> a big pile of coal with two wheelbarrows. Upstage
> right, a glimpse of the blue sea.]*
>
> *Two* COAL-CARRIERS, *stripped to the waist,
> their faces, hands and the naked parts of their bodies
> all black, sit on their wheelbarrows in despair. The*
> DAUGHTER *and* ADVOCATE *watch them from up-
> stage.*

DAUGHTER: This is Paradise!

FIRST COAL-CARRIER: This is hell!

SECOND COAL-CARRIER: Ninety in the shade.

[FIRST COAL-CARRIER: Shall we have a swim?

SECOND COAL-CARRIER: They'd arrest us. We're not
allowed to bathe here.

FIRST COAL-CARRIER: Couldn't we pick some of those
oranges?

SECOND COAL-CARRIER: They'd arrest us.]

FIRST COAL-CARRIER: I can't work in this heat. I'm
giving it up.

SECOND COAL-CARRIER: Then [they'll arrest you.
[*Pause.*] And] you'll have no food.

FIRST COAL-CARRIER: No food? We who work most
must eat least; and the rich who do nothing, they get most.
[Don't it seem a bit unjust? What do you think, Daughter
of God?]

DAUGHTER: Tell me. What have you done that you are so
black and your lot so hard?

FIRST COAL-CARRIER: What have we done? We were born of poor and not very good parents. Maybe got punished once or twice.

DAUGHTER: Punished?

FIRST COAL-CARRIER: Yes. The unpunished sit up there in the casino and eat eight courses with wine.

[DAUGHTER [to ADVOCATE]: Can this be true?

ADVOCATE: Broadly speaking, yes.

DAUGHTER: You mean that every human being has at some time done something deserving of imprisonment?

ADVOCATE: Yes.

DAUGHTER: You too?

ADVOCATE: Yes.

DAUGHTER: Is it true that these poor men are not allowed to bathe here?

ADVOCATE: Not even with their clothes on. Only those who have tried to drown themselves escape a fine. And they get a thrashing in the police station.

DAUGHTER: Couldn't they go outside the town and bathe somewhere in the countryside?

ADVOCATE: There isn't any countryside, it's all enclosed.

DAUGHTER: I mean in the common land.

ADVOCATE: There isn't any common land. It's all privately owned.

DAUGHTER: Even the sea?

ADVOCATE: Everything. You can't take a boat out or step ashore without paying for it. Pretty, eh?

DAUGHTER: This is not Paradise.

ADVOCATE: I assure you it isn't.]

DAUGHTER: But why do people do nothing to improve their lot?

ADVOCATE: Oh, some do. But all the improvers end in prison or the madhouse.

DAUGHTER: Who puts them in prison?

ADVOCATE: All right-thinking men, all honourable —

DAUGHTER: Who puts them in the madhouse?

ADVOCATE: Their own despair at the hopelessness of endeavour.

DAUGHTER: Does no one suspect that there may be some secret reason why things must be as they are?

ADVOCATE: Yes, the ones who are well off always think that.

DAUGHTER: That life is good as it is — ?

FIRST COAL-CARRIER: And yet we are society's corner-stone. If you didn't get any coal carried, the stove would go out in the kitchen, the fire in the living-room, the machine would stop in the factory; then the lights would go out in the streets, in the shops, in the home; darkness and cold would descend on you. And so we sweat in hell. What do *you* give us?

[ADVOCATE [*to* DAUGHTER]: Help them. [*Pause.*] I know everyone can't be totally equal, but need they be so unequal?]

    A GENTLEMAN *and his* WIFE *pass across the stage.*

WIFE: Do you feel like playing cards?

GENTLEMAN: No, I must take a walk to be able to eat lunch.

FIRST COAL-CARRIER: To be *able* to eat lunch?

[SECOND COAL-CARRIER: To be *able* — ?

    CHILDREN *enter and scream at the sight of the blackened workers.*

FIRST COAL-CARRIER: They scream at the sight of us.
They scream.]

SECOND COAL-CARRIER: God damn it! It's time to
bring out the knives and operate on this rotten body.

[FIRST COAL-CARRIER: God damn them! [*Spits.*]]

ADVOCATE [*to* DAUGHTER]: Mad, isn't it? People aren't
so bad. It's just —

DAUGHTER: Just?

ADVOCATE: The way things are run.]

DAUGHTER [*hides her face as she goes.*]: This is not
Paradise.

[COAL-CARRIERS: No. It is hell.]

Fingal's Cave. Long green waves lap slowly in. [*Downstage, a red bell-buoy rocks on the water, though it is
not heard except when indicated.*] *Music of the winds.
Music of the waves. The* DAUGHTER *and the* POET
enter.

POET: Where have you led me?

DAUGHTER:
Far from the hum and wailing of mankind,
To the limit of the world, this grotto which
We call the Ear of Indra, since the Lord
Of heaven hearkens here to man's complaints.

[POET: Here? How?

DAUGHTER:
Do you not see this cave is built like a shell?
Do you not know your ear is shaped like a shell?
You do, but have not considered it.
    [*Picks up a shell from the shore.*]
When you were a child, did you never hold
A shell to your ear and hear your heart's blood sigh,

Your thoughts whisper in your brain,
A thousand worn knots snap in the web of your body?
You hear that in this tiny shell. Imagine
How it must sound in this far greater one!]

POET [*listens*] : I hear nothing but the sighing of the winds.

DAUGHTER:
Let me interpret. Listen! The winds' complaint.
    [[*Soft music.*]]
Born in the broad abyss of heaven
We were sent by Indra's lightning
Down to dusty earth.
[The field-mud soiled our feet. We had to endure
The highway's dust, the city smoke, foul breaths,
The stink of food, the fumes of wine. We soared
Over the broad sea to cleanse our lungs,
Shake our wings, wash our feet.] O Indra, Lord
Of Heaven, hear us! Hear us when we sigh!
The earth is not clean. Life is not good.
Men are not evil. Nor are they good.
They live as they can, a day at a time. The sons
Of dust in dust must wander. Born of dust
To dust they return. They were given feet to plod,
Not wings. They grow dusty. Is the fault theirs or
yours?

[POET: I heard this once —

DAUGHTER:
Hush! The winds sing still —
    [*Soft music.*]]
We are winds, the air's children.
We carry the complaints of men.
Did you hear us
In the chimney on autumn evenings,
In the cracks of the stove, the gap in the window
When the rain wept outside on the tiles,
Or on winter evenings in snowy forests?
On the gale-swept sea, did you hear our wails and
    weeping

In the sails and in the rigging?
We are the winds, the air's children.
The human breasts through which we passed
Taught us these notes of sorrow.
In sickrooms, battlefields and, especially,
Nurseries where new-born babies wail and cry
At the pain of being born, that is us, us,
The winds that whistle and lament.
[Alas! Alas! Alas!

POET: I seem to have heard this once —

DAUGHTER:
Hush! The waves sing.
  [*Soft music.*]
It is we, we, the waves,
That rock the winds to rest. Green cradles are we.
Wet and salt, we are like tongues of fire
Quenching, burning, cleansing, bathing, begetting,
Conceiving. We, we, the waves,
That rock the winds to rest.]
False waves and faithless, all that is not burned
On earth is drowned — in the waves. See here.
  [[*Points to a heap of flotsam.*]]
See what the sea has plundered and destroyed.
[Only the figureheads of the sunk ships remain,
And their names — *Justice, Friendship, The Golden
Peace, Hope.* That is all that remains of Hope.
Treacherous Hope. Rockweed, rowlocks, bailers —
And see! The lifebuoy. He saved himself but let
The mariners perish.]

POET [*gropes among the flotsam*]:
Here is the name-board of the good ship *Justice*,
That left Fairhaven with the Blind Man's son.
So it has sunk. And there on board
Was Alice's lover, Edith's hopeless love.

DAUGHTER: The Blind Man? Fairhaven? I must have
dreamed that. And Alice's lover and ugly Edith. Foulstrand and the quarantine, sulphur and carbolic, the

ceremony in the church, the Advocate's office, the corridor
and Victoria, the rising castle and the Officer — I
dreamed it all.

POET: I wrote it.

DAUGHTER: Then you know what poetry is —

POET: Then I know what dreaming is. What is poetry?

DAUGHTER: Not reality, but greater than reality. No
dream, but waking dreams.

[POET:
    And mortals think we poets only play,
    Invent and fabricate.

DAUGHTER:
    It is better so, my friend. Else would the earth
    Lie waste for lack of encouragement.
    Men would lie on their backs and look at heaven.
    No man would take his turn with plough or spade,
    Plane or pickaxe.

POET:
    You say that, Indra's Daughter,
    You who are of the gods?

DAUGHTER:
    You are right to reproach me.
    I have been down here too long, bathing like you
    In mud. My thoughts can no longer fly.
    Clay on my wings; earth on my feet; and I — ! [*Raises
        her arms.*]
    I sink, sink. Help me, Father, O God of Heaven!
        [*Silence.*]
    I can no longer hear him. The ether
    No longer bears his speech to my ear's shell.
    The silver thread has snapped. Ah! I am earthbound!

POET: Will you leave us soon?

DAUGHTER: As soon as I have burned this flesh. The
ocean cannot cleanse me. Why do you ask?

POET: Because I have a boon to ask. A petition —

DAUGHTER: What kind of petition?

POET: A petition from mankind to the Master of the
world, written by a dreamer.

DAUGHTER: To be presented to him by — ?

POET: By Indra's daughter.

DAUGHTER: Can you speak your poem?

POET: I can.

DAUGHTER: Speak it, then.

POET: Better that you should.

DAUGHTER: Where shall I read it?

POET: In my thoughts. Or here. [*Hands her a scroll of
paper.*]

DAUGHTER: Very well. I shall speak it. [*Takes the paper,
but speaks the words without looking at it.*]
      "Why were you born in pain?
      Why do you torment your mother,
      Child of man, when you should give her
      The joy of motherhood, the greatest of all joys?
      Why do you awake to life?
      Why do you greet the light
      With a cry of hostility and pain?
      Why don't you smile at life,
      Child of man, since the gift of life
      Is meant to be joy itself?
      Why are we born like the beasts,
      We children of the gods and men?
      Our spirit craved another dress
      Than this of blood and dirt.
      Will God's image change its form?"
      Hush! A creation should not censure its maker.
      No one has yet solved the riddle of life.
      "And so begins our pilgrimage

Over thistles, thorns and stones.
Wherever the track is beaten, it is forbidden.
If you pluck a flower, it belongs to someone else.
If the road is blocked by a field and you must go on,
You tread on others' crops.
Then others tread on yours to even matters.
Every joy that you have brings grief to others,
But your grief brings joy to none.
So grief follows grief,
So goes the journey until your death,
Which other men will harvest."
Son of dust, is it thus you would approach the Highest?

POET:
How shall the son of dust find words
Light, clean and simple enough to rise from earth?
Child of God, will you translate our complaint
Into words more fitting for the ears of the Eternal One?

DAUGHTER: I will.

POET [*indicates the buoy*] : What is that floating there? A
buoy?

DAUGHTER: Yes

POET: It is like a lung with a windpipe.

DAUGHTER: It is the watchman of the sea. When danger
is near, it sings.

POET: The sea seems to be rising. The waves thunder.

DAUGHTER: It is so.

POET: Ah! What is that? A ship — on the reef!

DAUGHTER: What ship can it be?

POET: I think it is the ghost ship.

DAUGHTER: What is that?

POET: The Flying Dutchman.

DAUGHTER: Him? Why is he punished so cruelly, and
why does he never come ashore?

POET: Because he has seven faithless wives.

DAUGHTER: Must he be punished for that?

POET: Yes. All right-thinking people condemned him.

DAUGHTER: Strange world! How can he be freed from his curse, then?

POET: Freed? One bewares of freeing —

DAUGHTER: Why?

POET: Because — no, it isn't the Dutchman! It's an ordinary ship, in distress. Why does the buoy make no sound? Look — the sea is rising, the waves run high. Soon we shall be imprisoned in this cave. Now the ship's bell is ringing. Soon we shall have another figurehead. Cry, buoy, do your work, watchman! [*The buoy sings a quadruple chord in fifths and sixths, like foghorns.*] The crew are waving to us. But we shall perish.

DAUGHTER: Do you not want to be liberated from the flesh?

POET: Of course I do. But not now. And not by water.

THE CREW [*sing, four-part*]: Christ! Have mercy on us!

POET: Now they are crying, and the sea is crying. But no one hears.

CREW [*as before*]: Christ! Have mercy!

DAUGHTER: Who is that going to them out there?

POET: Walking on the water? There is only One Who walks on water. It cannot be Peter, the rock, for he sank like a rock.

A white light is visible out at sea.

CREW: Christ have mercy!

DAUGHTER: Is this He?

POET: It is He, the crucified —

DAUGHTER: Why — tell me, why was He crucified?

POET: Because He wished to liberate mankind.

DAUGHTER: Who — I have forgotten — Who crucified Him?

POET: All right-thinking people.

DAUGHTER: What a strange world!

POET: The sea is rising. Darkness is falling on us. The storm is rising. [*The* CREW *scream.*] The crew is crying with fear, now they see their Saviour. And now — they are jumping overboard, in fear of the Saviour. [*They scream again.*] Now they are crying because they have to die. They cry when they are born and they cry when they die.

The rising waves threaten to drown them in the cave.

DAUGHTER: If I were sure that it was a ship —

POET: In truth — I do not think it is a ship. It is a two-storeyed house, with trees outside. And a telephone tower — a tower that reaches into the clouds. It is a modern Tower of Babel, sending wires into the sky to communicate with the higher powers —

DAUGHTER: Child of man, human thought needs no metal threads to transmit it. The prayers of the godly instantly penetrate the ether. It is no Tower of Babel. If you would storm heaven, storm it with your prayers.

POET: No. It is no house, no telephone tower. Do you see?

DAUGHTER: What do you see?

POET: I see a snow-covered heath, a training-ground. The winter sun shines behind a church on the hill, and its spire casts its long shadow on the snow. Now a troop of soldiers comes marching. They march on the church, they climb the spire. Now they have reached the cross, but I sense that the first man to tread on the weathercock must die. Now they are nearing it — the corporal at their head — [*Laughs.*] A cloud passes over the heath, it blots out the sun — now everything is gone. The cloud's water quenched the sun's fire. The sun's light created the silhouette of the spire, but the silhouette of the cloud blotted out that of the tower.]

During this time, the scene has changed to the theatre corridor.

DAUGHTER [*to* STAGE-DOOR KEEPER]: Has the Lord Chancellor come yet?

STAGE-DOOR KEEPER: No.

DAUGHTER: Or the Deans?

STAGE-DOOR KEEPER: No.

DAUGHTER: Then call them at once, the door is to be opened.

STAGE-DOOR KEEPER: Is that so important?

DAUGHTER: Yes, it is. People feel that the solution to the riddle of existence lies hidden there. So call the Lord Chancellor and the Deans of the four faculties. [*The* STAGE-DOOR KEEPER *blows a whistle.*] And don't forget the glazier with the diamond, or we can't open it.

The theatre personnel enter left, as at the beginning of the play. Also, upstage, the OFFICER *in morning-coat and top-hat, with a bouquet of roses in his hand radiantly happy.*

OFFICER: Victoria!

STAGE-DOOR KEEPER: She'll be down in a moment.

OFFICER: That is good. The carriage is waiting, the table is laid, the champagne on ice. May I embrace you, madam? [*Embraces the* STAGE-DOOR KEEPER.] Victoria!

A WOMAN'S VOICE [*sings from above*]: I am here!

OFFICER [*begins to wander around*]: Good. I'll wait.

POET: I think I have seen this before.

DAUGHTER: I too.

POET: Perhaps I dreamed it?

DAUGHTER: Or wrote it, perhaps?

POET: Or wrote it.

DAUGHTER: Then you know what poetry is.

POET: Then I know what dreaming is.

DAUGHTER: I feel we stood somewhere else and spoke these words.

POET: Then you can soon work out what reality is.

DAUGHTER: Or dreaming.

POET: Or poetry.

> The LORD CHANCELLOR *and the* DEANS *of the faculties of Theology, Philosophy, Medicine and Law enter.*

CHANCELLOR: It's this question of the door, of course. What do you think, Dean of Theology?

[DEAN OF THEOLOGY: I do not think, I believe.

DEAN OF PHILOSOPHY: I rationalize —

DEAN OF MEDICINE: I *know* —

DEAN OF LAW: I doubt, until I have proof, with witnessess.

CHANCELLOR: Now they're going to quarrel again. Dean of Theology, what is your opinion?]

DEAN OF THEOLOGY: I believe that this door should not be opened. It conceals dangerous truths.

DEAN OF MEDICINE: Truth is never dangerous.

DEAN OF PHILOSOPHY: What is truth?

DEAN OF LAW: That which can be proved by two witnesses.

DEAN OF THEOLOGY: Anything can be proved with two witnesses by a law-twister.

DEAN OF PHILOSOPHY:[Truth is wisdom, and wisdom, which is knowledge, is philosophy.] Philosophy is the science of sciences, the knowing of knowledge, and all other sciences are philosophy's servants.

DEAN OF MEDICINE: [The only science is natural science.] Philosophy is not a science. It is merely barren speculation.

DEAN OF THEOLOGY: Bravo!

DEAN OF PHILOSOPHY [to DEAN OF THEOLOGY]: You say bravo. [What are you?] Your sort have always been the enemies of knowledge. [You are the contradiction of science, you are ignorance and darkness —]

DEAN OF MEDICINE: Bravo!

DEAN OF THEOLOGY [to DEAN OF MEDICINE]: You say bravo, you, who can't see further than your magnifying glass. [You only believe in your treacherous senses, your eyes which may be long-sighted, short-sighted, blind, dim, squinting, one-eyed, colour-blind, red-blind, green-blind —]

DEAN OF MEDICINE: Idiot!

DEAN OF THEOLOGY: Donkey! [*They start fighting.*]

[CHANCELLOR: Quiet! No need for the pot to call the kettle black!

DEAN OF PHILOSOPHY: If I had to choose between these two, Theology and Medicine, I'd choose — neither of them.]

DEAN OF LAW: [And if I had to judge between you three, I'd condemn you all. You can't agree on a single issue, and have never been able to. But to the point.] My Lord Chancellor, what is your opinion regarding this door and whether it should be opened?

CHANCELLOR: Opinion? [I have no opinions. I am merely appointed by the government to see that you don't break each other's arms and legs during your deliberations as how best to educate the young.] No, I beware of opinions. I had some once, but they were immediately refuted. Opinions are always immediately refuted — by one's opponent, of course. Perhaps we may open the door now, even at the risk that it may conceal dangerous truths?

DEAN OF LAW: What is truth? [Where is truth?]

DEAN OF THEOLOGY: I am the truth and the life —

DEAN OF PHILOSOPHY: I am the knowing of knowledge—

DEAN OF MEDICINE: I am the exact science.

[DEAN OF LAW: I doubt —

They start fighting.

DAUGHTER: Teachers of the young, you should be ashamed!

DEAN OF LAW: My Lord Chancellor, representative of the government, supremo of all teachers, punish this woman's presumption! She told you to be ashamed, which is an insult, and in a sneering and ironic tone she called you the teacher of the young, which is a slander.

DAUGHTER: Alas for the young!

DEAN OF LAW: She pities the young; that is the same as accusing us. My Lord Chancellor, punish her presumption.

DAUGHTER: Yes, I accuse you, all of you, of sowing doubt and discord in the minds of the young.

DEAN OF LAW: Listen to her! She arouses doubt of our authority in the minds of the young, and accuses us of sowing it! Is not this a criminal offence? I appeal to all right-minded people.

ALL RIGHT-MINDED PEOPLE: Yes, it is criminal.

DEAN OF LAW: All right-minded people have condemned you. Go in peace with your winnings. Otherwise —

DAUGHTER: My winnings? Otherwise — ? Otherwise what?

DEAN OF LAW: Otherwise you will be stoned.

POET: Or crucified.

DAUGHTER: I will go. Come with me, and you will learn the answer to the riddle.

POET: What riddle?

DAUGHTER: What does he mean by "my winnings"?

POET: Probably nothing. It's what we call talk. He was just talking.

DAUGHTER: But he hurt me deeply by saying it.

POET: That's why he said it. Such are mortals.]

ALL RIGHT-MINDED PEOPLE: Hurrah! The door is opened!

CHANCELLOR: What is hidden behind the door?

GLAZIER: I can't see anything.

CHANCELLOR: He can't see anything, no, very likely! Deans! What is hidden behind the door?

DEAN OF THEOLOGY: Nothing! That is the solution of the riddle of existence. Out of nothing in the beginning God created heaven and earth.

DEAN OF PHILOSOPHY: Nothing will come of nothing.

DEAN OF LAW: I doubt that. A fraud has been committed here. I appeal to all right-thinking persons!

DAUGHTER [to POET]: Who are right-thinking persons?

POET: Yes, answer who can! All right-thinking persons usually means just one person. Today it is I and mine, tomorrow you and yours. One gets nominated, or rather one nominates oneself.

ALL RIGHT-THINKING PEOPLE: We have been betrayed!

CHANCELLOR: Who has betrayed you?

ALL RIGHT-THINKING PEOPLE: Indra's daughter!

CHANCELLOR [to DAUGHTER]: Will you kindly tell us what you meant by opening this door?

[DAUGHTER: No, my good friends. If I told you, you wouldn't believe me.

DEAN OF MEDICINE: But there is nothing there.

DAUGHTER: Exactly. But you don't understand.

DEAN OF MEDICINE: She is talking bosh.

ALL: Bosh!]

DAUGHTER [to POET]: Poor people!

[POET: You are serious?

DAUGHTER: Always serious.]

POET: Even the right-thinkers?

DAUGHTER: They most of all.

[POET: And the four faculties too?

DAUGHTER: Them too, and not least. Four heads, four senses, one body! Who created that monster?]

ALL: She doesn't answer!

CHANCELLOR: Beat her, then.

DAUGHTER: I have answered.

CHANCELLOR: Listen, she is answering.

ALL: Beat her! She's answering!

[DAUGHTER: Whether she answers or does not answer — beat her! Come, seer, and far from here I will explain the riddle to you — but out in the wilderness, where no one will hear us, no one will see us. For —]

ADVOCATE [comes to her and takes her by the arm]: Have you forgotten your duties?

DAUGHTER: Oh, God, no! [But I have higher duties.

ADVOCATE: And your child?

DAUGHTER: My child? What more?]

ADVOCATE: Your child is crying for you.

DAUGHTER: My child! [Alas, I am earthbound.] This barb in my breast. This pain — what is it?

ADVOCATE: Don't you know?

DAUGHTER: No.

ADVOCATE: It is the pangs of conscience.

DAUGHTER: Is this the pangs of conscience?

ADVOCATE: Yes. And they come after [every neglected duty, every joy, even the most innocent. If there are any innocent joys, which is doubtful. And after] every suffering one inflicts on the person one loves.

DAUGHTER: And there is no cure?

ADVOCATE: Yes, but only one. It is, immediately to perform one's duty —

DAUGHTER: You look like a demon when you say that word "duty". [But when one has two duties to fulfil, as I have?

ADVOCATE: Then you must fulfil first one, then the other.

DAUGHTER: The highest first. Then, my dearest, look after my child, and I shall fulfil my duty.]

ADVOCATE: Your child misses you. Can you understand that a human being is suffering for you?

DAUGHTER: Now I feel discord in my soul. I have broken in two. I am tearing apart!

ADVOCATE: That is life's small disharmonies — you see?

DAUGHTER: Ah, how it tears me!

[POET: If you could guess how I have spread grief and destruction through fulfilling my calling — yes, my calling! — which is one's highest duty — would you not be willing to grasp my hand?

DAUGHTER: How do you mean?

POET: I had a father who built his hopes on me as his only son who would carry on his business. I ran away from business school. My father grieved himself to death. My mother wanted me to become a priest. I couldn't. So she rejected me. I had a friend who supported me when things were hardest. This friend then emerged as a tyrant against those for whom I spoke and sang. I had to reject this friend and benefactor to save my soul. Since then I have had no peace. People call me infamous, scum; it doesn't help that my conscience says; "You have done right", because in the next instant that same conscience tells me; "You have done wrong". Such is life.

DAUGHTER: Come with me into the wilderness.

ADVOCATE: Your child!

DAUGHTER [indicating everyone present] : These are my children. Each of them is good when alone, but once they meet they fight and become demons. Goodbye.

> Outside the castle. The decor is as at the beginning of the play. But the earth at the foot of the castle is now covered with flowers — blue monk's-hoods. On the top of the castle roof, on the glass lantern, can be seen a chrysanthemum bud ready to open. The castle windows are illuminated by candles. The DAUGHTER and the POET.]

DAUGHTER: The moment is nigh when, consumed with fire, I shall rise again into the ether. That is what you call death and which you approach with fear.

POET: Fear of the unknown.

DAUGHTER: Which you know.

POET: Who knows it?

DAUGHTER: Everyone. Why don't you believe your prophets?

[POET: Prophets have always been mistrusted. Why is that? And "if God has spoken, why do people not believe?" His word should be irresistible.

DAUGHTER: Have you always doubted?

POET: No. I have often felt certain. But after a while, my certainty always departed, like a dream when one awakes.

DAUGHTER: It is not easy to be a mortal.

POET: You see it, and admit it?

DAUGHTER: Yes.

POET: Tell me. Was it not Indra who once sent his son to earth to listen to man's complaints?

DAUGHTER: It was. How was he received?

POET: How did he perform his mission — to answer with a question?

DAUGHTER: To answer with another — was not man's condition bettered after his visit? Answer truthfully.

POET: Bettered? Yes, a little. Very little. But instead of asking, will you answer me the riddle?

DAUGHTER: Yes, but to what purpose? You will not believe me.

POET: I will believe you, for I know who you are.

DAUGHTER: Well, I will tell you. In the morning of time, before the sun shone, Brahma, the divine primal force, allowed Maja, the world mother, to induce him to multiply himself. This contact between the divine element and the earthly element was heaven's sin. Thus it is that the world, life, and mankind are but a phantom, an illusion, a dream vision —

POET: My dream!

DAUGHTER: A true dream. But to be liberated from the earthly element, Brahma's descendants crave privation and suffering. So, suffering is the liberator. But this need for suffering conflicts with the human desire for pleasure, and with love. Do you yet understand what love, is, with its sharpest joys inseparable from sharpest suffering, happiest when it is most bitter? Do you yet understand what woman is? Woman, through whom sin and death entered into life?

POET: I understand. And the end?

DAUGHTER: That you know. The strife between the agony of ecstasy and the ecstasy of agony. The pangs of the penitent and the joys of voluptuousness.

POET: Strife, then?

DAUGHTER: Strife between opposites generates power, just as fire and water generate steam.

POET: But peace? Rest?

DAUGHTER: Hush! You must ask no more and I may not reply.] The altar is already decked for the sacrifice. The flowers stand guard — the candles are lit — the white sheets cover the windows — the fir-twigs lie in the porch —

[POET: You say this as calmly as though suffering did not exist for you.

DAUGHTER: Not exist? I have suffered all your torments a hundredfold, for my perceptions were finer —

POET: Tell me your sorrows.

DAUGHTER: Poet, if you could tell me yours, and there was a word for every grief, could your words ever match the truth?

POET: No, you are right. To myself, I always seemed like a deaf-mute, and when the mob listened in wonder to my

song it sounded to me like discord. That is why I was
always ashamed when men praised me.

DAUGHTER: And you want *me* to? Look me in the eyes.

POET: I cannot endure your glance.

DAUGHTER: Then how could you endure my words, if I
spoke my tongue?]

POET: Tell me before you go. What did you suffer from
most down here?

DAUGHTER: From — being human. From feeling my sight
weakened by eyes, my hearing muffled by ears, and my
thought, my light, airy thought, cabined by the windings
of a brain. [You have seen a brain — what twistings, what
rat-holes!

POET: Yes. And that is why all right-thinking people
think twistedly.

DAUGHTER: Cruel, always cruel. But you all are.

POET: How can one be otherwise?]

DAUGHTER: Now at last I shake the dust from my feet —
the earth, the clay. [*Takes off her shoes and puts them in
the fire.*]

STAGE-DOOR KEEPER [*enters and puts her shawl in the
fire*]: Perhaps I may burn up my shawl too? [[*Goes.*]]

OFFICER [*enters*]: And I my roses, which have nothing
left but thorns. [[*Goes.*]]

BILL-POSTER [*enters*]: My posters can go, but my fishing-
net, never. [[*Goes.*]]

GLAZIER [*enters*]: My diamond, that opened the door.
Farewell. [[*Goes.*]]

ADVOCATE [*enters*]: The great lawsuit of the Pope's
beard, or the depletion of the sources of the Ganges.
[[*Goes.*]]

QUARANTINE MASTER [*enters*] : A mite, the black mask which made me a blackamoor against my will. [[*Goes.*]]

VICTORIA [*enters*] : My beauty, my sorrow. [[*Goes.*]]

EDITH [*enters*] : My ugliness, my sorrow. [[*Goes.*]]

> *Enter the* DANDY *in his wheelchair, with the* COQUETTE *and her* "FRIEND".

THE DANDY: Hurry, hurry, life is short! [[*Goes out with the others.*]]

POET: I have read that when life approaches its end, everything and everyone rushes past in a single stream. Is this the end?

DAUGHTER: Yes, it is mine. Goodbye.

POET: Say something to us.

DAUGHTER: No, I can't. Do you think your words could express our thoughts?

[DEAN OF THEOLOGY [*enters, in a rage*] : I am rejected by God, I am persecuted by men, rejected by the government and mocked by my fellows. How can I believe, when no one else believes? How shall I defend a God who will not defend His own? It's all bosh! [*Throws a book on the fire and goes.*]

POET [*takes the book from the fire*] : Do you know what this is? A book of martyrs, a calendar with a martyr for every day in the year.

DAUGHTER: Martyr?

POET: Yes, one who has been tortured and killed for his beliefs. Tell me why! Do you believe that all who are tortured suffer, that all who are killed feel pain? Suffering is the release, and death the liberator.]

KRISTIN [*enters with strips of paper*] : I'm pasting, I'm pasting, till there's nothing left to paste.

POET: And if heaven itself cracked, you would try to paste that together. Go!

KRISTIN: Have you no double windows in your castle then?

POET: No, Kristin, not there.

KRISTIN [*goes*]: Then I'll go, then.

DAUGHTER:
Our parting is at hand, the end approaches.
Farewell, you child of man, you dreamer,
You poet who best knowest how to live.
Hovering on wings above the earth
You plunge occasionally into the mire
To shake it from your feet, not to stick fast.
[Now I am going —] In the moment of goodbye,
When one must be parted from a friend, a place,
How suddenly great the loss of what one loved,
Regret for what one shattered.
[Oh, now I feel the agony of existence!
So this is to be mortal.]
One even misses what one did not value.
One even regrets crimes one did not commit.
One wants to go, and one wants to stay.
The twin halves of the heart are wrenched asunder
And one is torn as between raging horses
Of contradictions, irresolution, discord .
[Farewell. Tell your brothers and sisters I shall
        remember them
In the place to which I return, and in your name
Shall set their griefs before the throne of God.
Farewell!

*She goes into the castle. Music. The backcloth is
illuminated by the burning castle, showing a wall of
human faces, enquiring, grieving, despairing. As the
castle burns, the bud on the roof bursts open into a
giant chrysanthemum.*]

Methuen World Classics
include

Jean Anouilh (two volumes)
John Arden (two volumes)
Arden & D'Arcy
Brendan Behan
Aphra Behn
Bertolt Brecht (six volumes)
Büchner
Bulgakov
Calderón
Čapek
Anton Chekhov
Noël Coward (seven volumes)
Eduardo De Filippo
Max Frisch
John Galsworthy
Gogol
Gorky
Harley Granville Barker
(two volumes)
Henrik Ibsen (six volumes)
Lorca (three volumes)

Marivaux
Mustapha Matura
David Mercer (two volumes)
Arthur Miller (five volumes)
Molière
Musset
Peter Nichols (two volumes)
Clifford Odets
Joe Orton
A. W. Pinero
Luigi Pirandello
Terence Rattigan
(two volumes)
W. Somerset Maugham
(two volumes)
August Strindberg
(three volumes)
J. M. Synge
Ramón del Valle-Inclán
Frank Wedekind
Oscar Wilde

ML   6/05